THE MODERN MEANING OF JUDAISM

THE MODERN MEANING
OF JUDAISM

ROLAND B. GITTELSOHN

COLLINS

Cleveland ● New York

MS: Judaism

Portions of this book appeared in *The Meaning of Judaism* by Roland B. Gittelsohn, Cleveland: The World Publishing Company, 1970.

Library of Congress Catalog Card Number 78-69972
ISBN 0-529-05640-2 (cloth)
ISBN 0-529-05486-8 (paper)

Published by William Collins + World Publishing Co., Inc.
2080 West 117th Street, Cleveland, Ohio 44111

FT 5486   Printed in the United States of America

To
ARI, RON, DIANE, *and* DANIEL
May Judaism be as precious to them
as it is to
their loving grandfather.

CONTENTS

FOREWORD

THE ANCIENT, honored faith of Judaism lies at the core of Western civilization. It is the wellspring of the most noble and revered concepts in the annals of mankind: belief in one God as creator and eternal guide, the dignity and worth of all human beings, and the primacy of justice, freedom, and equality. Not only has Judaism had the distinction, as the world's first monotheism, of having given both impetus and direction to its sister faiths, Christianity, nineteen and more centuries ago, and Islam, six hundred years later; it has also bequeathed to the world the lore and literature of the Hebrew Scriptures, one of the most remarkable collections of writings in all history.

The origins of Judaism, as this book clearly outlines, can be traced to the geographic region of the Middle East and to a time period dating back at least 3,500, perhaps 4,000 years; the power, the inspiration that made it so significant and spread its influence so widely throughout the centuries endow it with unique worth and spiritual authority in these latter decades of the twentieth century. Judaism today has profound meaning for many millions and makes an extraordinary impact as important and far reaching as—perhaps even more so than—in the days of the patriarchs and the judges, the Psalmist and the eighth- and seventh-century prophets.

In Judaism, the eternal enters time, our very real present, and offers the timeless Word as guidance amid the stresses and problems of our day. This volume, so felicitously crafted by Roland B. Gittelsohn, offers both information and insight regarding the nature of Judaism today.

Dr. Gittelsohn is well known as a rabbi and scholar, a civic leader and national figure. His foremost position in American Judaism and his achievements in the interfaith and ecumenical movements qualify him admirably to write on the subject, *The Modern Meaning of Judaism*.

Most vivid and compelling are his descriptions of the great tragedy and the great triumph of the Jewish people in the twentieth century—the Holocaust and the establishment of Israel. He enables us to share the pain and grief of a venerated people, as they endured the martyrdom of the six million; and their joy in the realization of a 1900-year-old dream, to establish a third Jewish commonwealth and restore to its former beauty and fertility the Land whence came the People and the Book. He ranges in his writing from the plight of refugees, both Jewish and Arab, and the ring of enmity that encircles modern Israel to the specific problems Judaism must help solve in our time.

These pages are the result of a lifetime of study, of constant reading and thought. Here the reader will find wisdom and courage, candor and truth. Roland Gittelsohn's *The Modern Meaning of Judaism* is a book with a message for all.

May 1978   CARL HERMANN VOSS

Carl Hermann Voss, editor of *The Modern Meaning of Judaism*, is Ecumenical Scholar-in-Residence on behalf of the National Conference of Christians and Jews.

INTRODUCTION

THE SCOPE SUGGESTED by the title of this book is beyond
any reasonable reach, for Judaism encompasses nearly four
thousand years of history, literature, language, music, art,
philosophical speculation, and faith. Scholars far more
competent that I have written heavy volumes—indeed, entire series of such—to illumine only limited aspects of the
whole.

My hope is a more modest one. If the reader can gain
from these pages a sensitivity to the totality of Jewish history and hope, a sense of the uniquenesses which constitute
Judaism, I shall have succeeded. If, in addition, his appetite
can be whetted to read more and learn more, my highest
hope will have been realized.

No claim is made for complete objectivity. I can no more
be utterly objective about Judaism than about my grand-
children. I love both. I am as firmly convinced as one can
be on such matters that had I been born without a religious
heritage, had I begun my quest for a meaningful orientation
to life only in my adult years and searched as scrupulously
as possible, I would have chosen Judaism as my own. It is
not the purpose of these pages to convince others that they
must reach the same conclusion. It will be enough if the non-
Jewish reader can be helped to understand why Judaism
means so much to me, and if the Jewish reader can be en-

couraged to appreciate that it should have no less significance for him.

I am profoundly persuaded that I need Judaism in order
to live on the highest levels my capacities will permit, and
that the world needs Judaism for what it has already contributed—and may yet contribute—to the sum total of civilization. Everything which follows will proceed from this
perspective.

A discussion can easily be divided into logical sections
and chapters. We must not expect, however, that a living
heritage will always be as neatly logical as a description of
it. It will become apparent soon enough that some backing
and filling will be required. Certain ethical emphases will
be included in my discussion of theology, while more than a
few theological matters will be interfused with my presenta-
tion of Jewish ethics. This would probably be true in the
exposition of any millennial tradition. For reasons which
will be clarified in our first chapter, it is even truer of
Judaism.

A final introductory word about sources, and we shall be
ready to proceed. The primary fountainheads of Judaism
are the Bible and the Talmud. Our Jewish Bible consists
of the thirty-nine books usually referred to by non-Jews as
the Old Testament; * we do not accept the "New Testament" of the Christian community as part of our sacred
scripture.

When our Bible became canonized at about the second
century B.C.E. ** (Before the Common Era), changing conditions and circumstances necessitated new legislation as
well as reinterpretation of many old laws. To meet these
post-biblical needs, the ancient rabbis created a large body
of law called the Mishnah, which was completed about 200
C.E. (Common Era). Every law in the Mishnah is based on

* See pp. 63-65.
** See p. 65.

previous biblical legislation. Because there was still need for reinterpretation and change, the laws of the Mishnah were subsequently discussed at length in the rabbinic academies. Eventually these discussions were also reduced to written form, known as the Gemarah. The Mishnah and Gemarah together constitute the Talmud.

All this—Bible, Mishnah, Gemarah, and even the many post-talmudic commentaries and codes are a continuing development of Jewish law and thought. Even today leading authorities on Judaism are adding to this never-ending evolution of a venerable yet living tradition. The Hebrew Bible and everything which has followed from it will be our principal sources as we inquire now into the modern meaning of Judaism.

PART ONE
WHAT THE JEW IS

CHAPTER ONE

Stars and Sand

By Myself I swear, the Lord declares: I will bestow My blessing upon you and make your descendants as numerous as the stars of heaven and the sands on the seashore . . .

Genesis 22:16f.

Rabbi Judah ben Ilai said:
   This people is compared to dust
   and it is compared to stars.
   When it sinks,
   it sinks into the very dust;
   when it rises,
   it rises to the very stars.

Talmud
Megillah 16a

Who is a Jew?

Simple question, isn't it? Especially for a rabbi who has spent his entire adult life working with and for Jews. No, it isn't simple at all. Much energy and effort—some of it agonized, none of it entirely conclusive—have been directed by Jews toward defining themselves.

Should we define a Jew as anyone who was born of Jewish parents? A few years ago a Catholic monk applied

for automatic citizenship in Israel. Born in Europe of Jewish parents, reared in earliest childhood as a Jew, Brother
Daniel had survived the Holocaust because of a Catholic
family that had courageously claimed him as its own. His
biological parents perished in Hitler's ovens.

Grateful to the couple who had saved him, educated in
their religious tradition, Brother Daniel had not only converted to their faith but had become a monk. He lives and
works in Israel. Under the Law of Return, which grants
immediate and automatic citizenship to every Jewish
immigrant who is not a fugitive from another nation's justice, he asked to be registered as a citizen.

Is Brother Daniel in fact a Jew? After pondering the
matter at great length, the Supreme Court of Israel said
"no," ruling that he is not entitled to acceptance under the
Law of Return. He became a citizen, but only by following
the lengthier procedure of formal application by which a
non-Jew acquires citizenship rather than claiming it
automatically.

Dorothy P. * was born and reared a Christian. Though
she felt mildly uncomfortable with certain aspects of
church doctrine, the thought of conversion to Judaism
didn't occur to her until after she had become engaged to
marry Harry, a Jew. Then, moved primarily by a desire for
her children to enjoy a religiously unified home, she studied Judaism and was converted to it. She has found its
teachings most congenial to her own disposition. Her zeal
for her new faith has been exemplary; she has served as an
officer of her congregation and both her children—now
adults—identify themselves as Jews. Her son, in fact, has
become a rabbi.

---

* Except for Brother Daniel and Franklin Littell, all names used in this
discussion are fictitious. The types of individuals described, however,
are drawn from real life.

Is Dorothy a Jew? If so, what becomes of the proposal that we define a Jew as one born of Jewish parents?

How about saying that a Jew is any person who accepts the faith of Judaism?

Zev E. and his wife Ilana are Israeli graduate students in the United States. When their studies here are completed, they expect to return to Israel. Both Zev and Ilana were born in Israel. Their parents had escaped from Nazi concentration camps and perilously made their way in the early 1940s to what was then called Palestine. The Holocaust which resulted in the murder of six million Jews had extinguished all remnants of Zev's and Ilana's religious faith. They do not believe in God, are affiliated with a synagogue neither in Israel nor here, and never pray. To them Judaism means belonging to a nation, a nation which had been dispossessed for centuries from its ancestral soil but has now returned. The preservation and protection of their State is the highest ideal they know.

They have both fought in Israel's wars. In the United States they work actively to support Israel because they believe that only a strong Israel can insure the worldwide survival of the Jewish people. Clearly, they do not accept Judaism as a religious faith. Are they Jews?

Is Harry F.? Many years have passed since he was last in a synagogue. He is a Hebrew teacher, well acquainted with the Bible and other works of traditional Jewish literature.

Harry agrees that religion has been a principal component of Judaism throughout its past development, but he has concluded that for Jews, as for all peoples, civilization has reached a point where religion is no longer needed. Having served its useful and necessary purposes, it is, he believes, already in the process of dissolution. "Modern science, technology, and philosophy can now accomplish more effectively for us the purposes served by religion for our ancestors," he contends. Hence he has dispensed with synagogue attendance and prayer.

Yet Harry considers himself to be a loyal Jew. He reads and teaches the Bible as a record of the national experience of the Jewish people; he still observes in his home certain Jewish holidays which symbolize and commemorate that national history; he retains those traditional rituals which he can interpret as Jewish folkways or mores and which reinforce his feeling of unity with other Jews.

Harry believes Judaism to be primarily a culture—a predominantly religious culture through much of the past, to be sure, but no less viable now in nonreligious terms. He therefore cherishes and teaches Jewish literature, music, and art and attends as many Jewish lectures and concerts as he can. He is convinced that Israel represents the most hopeful center for the preservation of past Jewish culture as well as the most fertile and receptive soil for continued Jewish creativity in the future. Is Harry a Jew?

Leon M. belongs to an Orthodox Jewish congregation. He believes that the Torah, the first five books of the Hebrew Bible, was revealed by God to Moses on Mt. Sinai, and that all subsequent Jewish religious truth, as expanded and expressed in post-biblical literature, is implicit in Hebrew Scripture.

Leon would define a Jew as one who agrees with his views and who practices the rituals and ceremonies of Judaism as they were prescribed in the Bible and Talmud. He eats only kosher foods, worships in the synagogue three times daily, and abstains from business and commercial activity on Saturday and all Jewish holidays. For him religious truth is eternal and unchanging. To tamper with divinely revealed truth is, he insists, colossal impudence.

Sam S. belongs to a Reform Jewish congregation. Jewish tradition is very important to him, but he is convinced that it must be reinterpreted in accordance with changing circumstances and needs. While he agrees with Leon M. that the Torah is a divinely inspired document, he adds that it was written by human beings and therefore contains some imperfections and errors along with its lofty and eternal truths. Where Leon says that God revealed the Torah, Sam asserts that the Torah reveals God.

Sam practices those rituals of traditional Judaism which in his judgment still have meaning for modern Jews. Others, however, which are no longer meaningful, he has rejected.*

Karl M. belongs to a small organization which calls itself "Jews for Jesus". Members of this group hold that Jesus was the fulfillment of biblical Judaism, the Messiah foretold by ancient Hebrew prophecy.

Karl and his friends call themselves Jewish Christians. Their religious services are an admixture of both Jewish and Christian liturgy. To them, Christian theology is the culmination of Jewish belief. Because they see Christianity as the logical, inevitable consequence of Judaism, they believe themselves to be the only true Jews and the only authentic Christians. They claim that other Jews are mistaken in not accepting Jesus as the Messiah, while Christians err in assuming that in order to embrace Jesus it is necessary to establish a religion other than Judaism.

You may be ready to decide which of the individuals already described are Jews, which are not. But we haven't yet covered the full range of possibilities. There are some Jews who aren't able to locate themselves comfortably in any of the foregoing categories. They say that whatever

* For further details on the differences between Orthodox and Reform Jews, see pages 22-25.

the perimeters of Jewish identification may have been in the past, today's circumstances require a different kind of definition.

They would therefore label as a Jew any person who supports the State of Israel as an indispensable prerequisite for Jewish survival.

Professor Franklin H. Littell of Temple University in Philadelphia is such a person. A Protestant minister, he has visited Israel more often than most rabbis, has studied and taught there in depth for long periods of time, has stimulated more Christian help for Israel in the United States than perhaps any other individual. Is he a Jew?

Is Mendel S.? He is a chasidic rabbi, living in the Williamsburg section of Brooklyn, New York. The chasidim were an eighteenth-century semimystical sect of Jews, originating in Poland, who stressed the joyous and emotional aspects of religious life in preference to its somber, intellectual moods. Those who call themselves chasidim in America today (very few in number) are only in part representative of what the movement was originally. To a greater degree they are the extremists among Orthodox Jews, holding staunchly to the old ways of practice and belief, rigidly resisting all change.

Mendel is an opponent of the Zionist movement, which since 1897 has promoted the establishment of a Jewish state. The birth of Israel in 1948 he considered to be sinful. Not that he disagreed with the biblical prophecy that one day all the scattered Jewish exiles would be gathered from the four corners of the earth to live in their ancient homeland again. But he believed this to be a divine prerogative, even as it had from the beginning been a divine promise. God would shepherd the Jewish people back to what had been Palestine in his own time and in his own mysterious way. For us to intervene, to use purely human means, to hurry the hand of God, as it were—this, to Mendel, was unforgivable arrogance.

It distresses Mendel enormously that so many Jews have suffered in Israel's wars. Yet he sees their pain almost as a kind of divine retribution. "Jews have no business employing political and military means to achieve ends which only God can order. We are strictly a religious group. Had we waited for God to effect the ingathering of exiles in His supernatural way, there would have been no trouble with the Arabs, no difficulty in the United Nations, no war or destruction or death."

Mendel isn't the only person who calls himself a Jew, yet vigorously opposes the State of Israel. Rose L. is a member of a very small organization called the American Council for Judaism. The basic tenet of this group has been opposition to Zionism and the State of Israel, opposition quite different from that of the chasidim. Members of the American Council do not see the return of Jews to their ancient homeland as a divine imperative at all; in fact, it betrays for them a gross misunderstanding of the nature and purpose of Judaism. They claim that Jews are strictly a religious group in the same sense that Roman Catholics or Presbyterians are. They look upon the creation of Israel as a return to a narrow nationalism which the Jewish people outgrew centuries ago.

Rose and her associates have always been convinced that there is no hope for Jews and Arabs to coexist in the Middle East. Some of the Council's leaders have even cooperated with Arab extremists in trying to sway world opinion against Israel. Rose resents the Israelis principally because she fears that their State implies that she holds dual loyalties and is not a completely patriotic American.

Who is a Jew?

Complicated question, isn't it? Can it be answered? Shall we define a Jew as anyone born of Jewish parents? Then how about Brother Daniel? Dorothy P.? Karl M.?

Is a Jew a person who subscribes to the faith of Judaism? What does this definition do to the Jewish identities of Zev and Ilana? Or Harry F.? Would Leon M. and Mendel S. call Sam S. a Jew? Would Sam agree that they and Zev and Ilana are Jews?

What about all those self-professing Jews who label themselves atheists? Judaism can be compressed into a religious category such as Methodism or Episcopalianism only by distorting both its history and its nature. There is no such thing as an atheistic Methodist or Episcopalian. One can be an atheist, however, and still be a Jew. One might thereby deny oneself the most meaningful dimension of Jewishness, but a definition of Judaism must include all Jews, not only those who participate most fully.

Shall we, then, define Judaism as nationalism and the Jewish people as a nationality? This would leave us with only Zev and Ilana as Jews. While the others may share with them many traits normally associated with nationhood—language, literature, history, culture, destiny, among others—only Zev and Ilana possess national ties to a Jewish state. All the others are—by nation, by civic, political, and military loyalty—Americans.

To define Judaism as a race would be to employ the most misleading and inaccurate term of all. Many anthropologists recommend that we drop the word *race* altogether; there is, they maintain, almost no such thing on earth as a pure race. Surely with regard to Jews the designation of race is worthless. Speaking racially, there are Semitic Jews, Caucasian Jews, Negro Jews, and Oriental Jews. In Israel one sees all of them within a few minutes or a few miles. Race must be the least likely common denominator among Jews.

If a Jew is one who supports Israel because he wants the Jewish people and their heritage to persist and he sees Israel as indispensable toward that end, is Franklin A. Littell a Jew? Mendel S.? Rose L.?

We might well disagree as to whether any given individual described in this chapter is or is not a Jew. Of one thing, however, we can be certain: whatever list any of us makes of those whom he or she would identify as Jewish, none of the definitions so far proposed would include them all. And no definition is acceptable which excludes any person whom we believe to be a Jew.

Our enemies seem to have less difficulty defining us than we Jews have defining ourselves. To Adolf Hitler a Jew was any person with even one Jewish great-grandparent! At the very moment when Israel was withdrawing from part of the Sinai peninsula in 1974, its parliament, the Knesset, was debating, "Who is a Jew?" A Hebrew inscription on one of the military trucks headed northward from Egypt read, "Who is a Jew? Sadat knows!"

Yet we ourselves still discuss and debate. The difficulty in defining Judaism emerges from the fact that we Jews constitute a unique group. None of the customary sociological or anthropological categories is a perfect fit. We are a religious group, true—but simultaneously more than that. We share some facets of national existence, but not all of us partake of them fully. The fact is that if we are to define ourselves with any substantial measure of accuracy and completeness, a new term must be invented. Martin Buber, renowned Jewish philosopher, came close to the crux of the matter when he wrote, "Israel is not one member of the species 'nation.' It is the only example of the species 'Israel'."[1] Buber's words regarding Israel as a State can be applied no less aptly to Jews as a worldwide entity.

Even in ancient times our people seem to have defied definition by the customary categories. The Hebrew term *le-um,* meaning "nation," is never applied to us in biblical literature;* *goy,* another word for "nation," is almost never used for Jews. In the Bible as in most post-biblical sources we are referred to as an *am,* a "people." Perhaps this is as close as one can come to an accurate definition of the Jewish group; it is a singular kind of people, in whose historic development religious and national elements have been inextricably interwoven. In our own time the director of the Hillel Foundation at the Hebrew University, Rabbi Jack J. Cohen, has suggested, "What was secular in other groups was religious among Jews. What was nationalistic in other groups was religious among Jews. Jewish religion was the core of their nationalism and culture."[2]

Another look at our cast of characters may help us to understand these apparent contradictions. Ilana and Zev profess no religious convictions at all; they might even be horrified at being designated as religious. If they are typical Israelis, however, they are more intimately familiar with the Bible, the Talmud, and the important medieval sources of Jewish thought than are many religious Jews in the United States.

Some years ago I participated on a panel of Jewish educators, my assignment being to speak for religiously oriented Jewish education. I listened with very special interest to the comments of another participant whose task was to urge the virtues of secularist Jewish education. He described the content of his school's curriculm as including study of the Torah, the Sabbath and other holidays, the ceremonies and rituals of Judaism. At one point he even disclosed that the literature taught in his school included the Jewish "dialogue with God." Secularist indeed!

A few years ago Moshe Dayan, the famous Israeli mili-

---

* Use of this word in Genesis 25:23, referring to the twins being carried by Rebecca, is scarcely a definitive description of the ancient Israelites.

tary and political leader, was interviewed by a French journalist. He confessed categorically: "I am not religious." Then, in two astonishing sentences, he added: "I know my history, and I want my children to be raised in this history. I want them to have a high opinion of it—not as concerns the religion, but as it concerns the philosophy of Judaism—justice, mercy, the equality of people and the idea that God made man in his own image."[3] So this is what it means for a Jew to be secular: the affirmation that God made human beings in his own image!

What all this adds up to is that historic Judaism has been neither religion nor nationalism exclusively, but rather religion and nationalism comprehensively. Like the fingers of my clasped hands, the religious and nationalistic elements of Judaism can be separated only by mutilating the whole of which they are part.

The fact that we cannot be limited to religious identification alone should not minimize the importance of religion as a major component, perhaps *the* major component of our peoplehood. This truth was apparent even at a time when there could be no doubt about our national status—namely, during the historic periods reflected in our Bible. After the division of the nation into two kingdoms which followed the death of Solomon, the two greatest monarchs of Judah and Israel are dismissed with fourteen verses in II Kings. The prophet Elijah, however, receives more than five chapters, while his successor, Elisha, occupies eight chapters.

It would not be inaccurate to suggest that religion has been to Judaism what the heart is to the human body. The heart is so much smaller than the body as to appear deceptively insignificant, yet, without the sustained pulsing of the heart the body could not endure. Without the infusion of energy and meaning from the religious impulse within Judaism, even those of its aspects which appear to be nonreligious would in the course of time vanish.

A modern political scientist has encapsulated this truth in the form of a parable from actual experience:

> A young man of my acquaintance was recently in Haifa. He saw an elderly and obviously Orthodox Jew coming towards him, and something in the man's face caught his fancy. When they drew near, my friend said, "Shalom Aleichem," and, evidently, said it. with a tone that is reserved for friends. The older man, returning the greeting, looked a bit puzzled, and asked, "Do I know you?" To which my friend answered, "Yes,—we met at Sinai." The older man slapped his head, and said, "Of course, I simply forgot. You'll have to forgive me—it was so crowded and noisy. How have you been?"[4]

Even if one attempts to describe authentic Jewish values without direct reference to theology or God, the essential core goes back to what Jews have always symbolized through the glimpses of divinity their ancestors received at Sinai.

Many years ago a well-known sociologist came about as close as anyone to answering the not-so-simple question of this chapter. After much speculation and study, Dr. Carl Mayer concluded: "The Jews, it may be said, are neither a nation nor a religious community in the usual sense of these words, rather they are both at the same time, in such a way as to make any distinction between these two concepts impossible. The nation is at its foundation a religious community, and the religious community is a nation."[5]

Rabbi Robert Gordis, a distinguished rabbi, teacher, and author agrees: "The Jewish people . . . cannot be placed in any of the usual classifications like 'race,' 'nation,' or 'nationality' without distorting the reality. If, nevertheless, we insist upon a modern sociological term, the Jews may be described as a religio-cultural-ethnic group."

The meaning today of this group and its heritage is the

concern of this book. We shall commence with theological attitudes, not only because they crystallize the most precious convictions and postulates of the Jewish people, but also because, in a peculiarly exciting and significant way, many Jews who call themselves atheists nevertheless subscribe in substantial measure to the values implicit in Jewish theology.

PART TWO
WHAT THE JEW BELIEVES

Essential Preliminaries

THEOLOGICAL SPECULATION as such has played a much less important role in Judaism than in most other religious approaches to life. Not that the Jew believed less in God. His observations of the universe and of his own history convinced him that there must be a creative, unifying, purposive Spiritual Core at the very heart of reality. This he assumed to be so. Then, rather than indulging in endless reflection on the exact nature of that Core, he proceeded to dwell instead on what It demanded of him ethically. When the prophet Micah summarized what the Lord required of those who believe in Him, he did not suggest that we must fully comprehend God. He urged only that we "do justly, love mercy and walk humbly with your God." Priority was given to the doing of justice and the loving of mercy. Only then could we approach the possibility of walking with God.

In the generation preceding Jesus, the great Jewish teacher Hillel was challenged by an impudent heathen to state the essence of Judaism while standing on one foot. With exemplary patience Hillel replied, "What is hateful to you, do not do to your fellow. All the rest is commentary; go, learn it." Again, no call to extended philosophizing about the deity. Rather the assumption that He exists, that He is beyond full human comprehension, that our primary obligation is to observe His ethical dictates.

An ancient rabbi expressed this Judaic emphasis in a bold and daring way. He was commenting on the verse in Jeremiah which reads: "They have forsaken Me and have not kept my Torah." He pictured God, as it were, saying, "Would that they forsake Me if only they keep my Torah, for had they occupied themselves with the Torah, the leaven which is in it would have brought them back to Me."[1] If we bear in mind that the Torah does not consist quintessentially of theological deliberation but of ethical admonition, we shall at once grasp the priority which Judaism has always given to ethics over theology.

Judaism does not begin with theology. It begins with the unique historic experience of a perdurable people. From that experience and our observations of nature, we Jews have arrived at certain principles and convictions which constitute our theology. Theology is thus the end result, not the initial impulse.

Here we come upon a crucial difference between Judaism and Christianity. R. Travers Herford, one of the greatest Christian authorities on ancient Judaism, has written: "Judaism . . . is a detailed system of ethical *practices* by which its adherents consecrated their daily lives to the *service* of God. The cornerstone of Judaism was the *deed*, not the *dogma*. The fundamental characteristic of Christianity, as it was preached by the apostles, and as it is embodied today in both the Protestant and the Catholic Churches, was, on the other hand, faith in a Person, that person being, of course, the Founder. 'Believe in the Lord Jesus,' says Christianity, 'and thou shalt be saved.' Salvation for professing Christians is not a consequence of duty done in the conscious service of God; it is something mystically received as a gift of divine grace. . . . Christianity and Judaism appealed to different sides of human nature; the former to the passive side, the latter to the active side. Christianity stressed *faith*, Judaism *right action*."[2]

This truth has been expressed poignantly in a chasidic parable. A drayman sought the advice of his rabbi on whether he should change his occupation because it interfered with regular attendance at the synagogue. The rabbi responded with a question: "Do you carry poor passengers free?" "Yes," answered the drayman. "Then," said the sage, "you serve the Lord as faithfully in your daily work as you would by more frequent worship in the synagogue." This should not be taken to mean that Judaism in any way disparages participation in public worship; we shall have more to say on that later. It does mean that Judaism places its highest priority on deed, not creed.

All that a religious Jew is expected to believe on faith about God can be summarized in a single sentence: God is one, He is purely spiritual, and He makes stringent ethical demands on us. Beyond this, there is the widest latitude for individual Jews to differ in their interpretations and understandings of God. Not even all rabbis are in exact agreement. They differ on whether God is personal and possesses consciousness. They vary in their views on revelation, on immortality, on prayer—on just about every matter of interpretation. So long as they accept the fact that God is one, spiritual and ethically demanding, their concept of deity is authentically Jewish.

Rabbi Mordecai Kaplan, a seminal thinker in modern Jewish life, expressed a very important truth about Jewish theology when he wrote, " . . . as far as Jewish religion . . . is concerned, it matters very little how we conceive God as long as we so believe in God that belief in Him makes a tremendous difference in our lives."

Judaism poses no creed to which each individual must subscribe. From time to time in the long course of Jewish development, individual rabbis suggested their own personal creeds, but none of these was ever accepted as compulsory for all Jews. In a theological sense Judaism might well be described as a climate of conviction rather than a creed. Within that general climate, there was always room for divergence of opinion.

Judaism has been spacious enough to accommodate both Maimonides, a severe rationalist, and Israel Baal Shem Tov,* a mystic who looked askance at the intellectual pursuit of God. Two thousand years ago the disciples of Hillel and of Shammai disagreed vigorously on many matters involving Jewish belief and practice. The Talmud resolved their disputes in typically Jewish fashion: "Both these and those are the words of the living God."

Today too there is significant religious disagreement within the household of Judaism. In the United States religious Jews are divided principally into Orthodox, Conservative, and Reform branches. The differences among them revolve more often around matters of ritual observance than of theological tenet. Orthodox Jews adhere to Judaism as it was practiced in talmudic times. Reform Jews stress the importance of adapting religious life to the spirit and mood of the modern age. Conservative Jews stand generally between the other two, holding to as much of ancient tradition as they can render compatible with today's needs.**

Worship in the Orthodox synagogue is entirely in Hebrew; men and women sit separately; heads are covered as a symbol of adoration and respect for God. The Conservative service is somewhat shortened; it is conducted about equally in Hebrew and English; heads are covered; men and women usually sit together. Reform worship is abbreviated even more; is conducted more in English than in Hebrew; the covering of heads is optional; men and women are always seated together. All Orthodox Jews are expected to keep the dietary laws prescribed in the Bible

* Founder of Chasidism in the eighteenth century; see p. 32.
** See p. 6f. concerning Leon Morris and Sam Stone.

and Talmud, the so-called laws of *kashrut*. Certain types of food are prohibited; animals must be slaughtered in a specified manner to be eligible for human consumption; meat and dairy foods may not be consumed during the same meal. In theory Conservative Jews are also obliged to observe these dietary laws, though often they honor them more in theory than in fact. While some Reform Jews do observe them, the majority do not.

There are no hard-and-fast lines of distinction among these contemporary divisions within Judaism. While it is easy to distinguish Orthodox from Reform congregations, Conservative groups cover a spectrum which, at its ends, closely resembles both of the other branches.

A small fourth group of religious Jews in the United States is known as Reconstructionists. They are the disciples of Rabbi Mordecai Kaplan. Bridging the gap between Conservative and Reform Judaism, their unique emphasis is on Judaism as a religious civilization rather than a religious faith *per se*, on the importance of Israel for Jews and Jewish life everywhere, and on naturalistic theology.* Though much smaller in numbers than any of the three major groups, the Reconstructionist frame of reference is highly significant because, to a considerable extent, it has been accepted by many Reform and Conservative Jews.

The division of Jewish religious life into these three branches is of recent origin. Contrary to popular impression, as an organized movement Reform Judaism is the oldest. Throughout Jewish history there have been numerous sects or groups which emphasized one or another phase of Judaism. Though they sometimes harbored considerable animosity toward one another, all were really bound within the tradition. There was, moreover, ample provision for both disagreement and flexibility. In every

* See p. 25.

age the rabbis were able to reinterpret religious law, continuously adapting it to new circumstances and problems. There was, therefore, no need for the three major interpretations which exist today.

A major change came with the French Revolution and the Napoleonic era. The ghetto walls began to crumble and, for the first time in most European lands, Jews were allowed to mingle economically, intellectually, and later socially, with Christians. The so-called Emancipation had commenced.

This had an immense impact upon Jewish life. Some Jews were so mesmerized by the new freedom that they rushed to abandon Judaism entirely. Others saw a need for rapid and radical adaptation if they were to remain Jews without surrendering either freedom or intellectual integrity. These were the founders of the Reform movement, which originated in Germany but reached its culmination in the United States.

While Emancipation enticed some Jews, it frightened others. They interpreted Reform as an entering wedge which threatened the eventual dissolution of Judaism and disappearance of the Jewish people. They therefore reacted against even the moderate rate of change which the tradition had always allowed. Their efforts led to the Orthodox movement.

Caught between these opposing trends were those Jews who agreed that adaptation and change were essential, but felt the Reformers were proceeding too far and too fast. They established Conservative Judaism in the hope of synthesizing the Orthodox Jew's love of tradition and respect for religious law with the Reform Jew's insistence on progressive adaptation. In a sense then, both Orthodoxy and Conservatism are reactions to Reform.

No one of these branches of Judaism is monolithic. Some Orthodox Jews are fanatically opposed to all change and rigidly devoted to the forms of their faith precisely as these have been handed down by previous generations. Others are more moderate, recognizing that some flexibility is necessary, but holding that it must be achieved only through the rather cumbersome procedures of the past. Conservative Jews, as we have already observed, may resemble either of the other varieties. Within Reform there are differences too: some insist that Reform Judaism must remain what it was in the nineteenth and early twentieth centuries; others—a substantial majority—are convinced that, like all movements of protest, Reform reacted to an extreme and must now achieve a more reasonable and moderate stance. Most Reform Jews today are more respectful of traditional ritual and the Hebrew language than were their predecessors. Their approach is a selective one; they believe in adhering to traditional patterns which retain meaning under modern conditions of life, while relinquishing those which have outlived their usefulness.

Orthodox, Conservative, Reconstructionist, and Reform—all are Jews. Believers and nonbelievers, religionists and secularists—Jews, all of them. The concept of *k'lal Yisra-ayl*—the community or totality of the Jewish people—is an extremely important one. Except for an extreme fringe within Orthodoxy, who believe that they alone are authentically Jewish, all Jews, regardless of how they differ among themselves, recognize that the whole is greater than the sum of its parts and that they belong, with variant interpretations of deity and destiny, to a single entity, the Jewish people.

Before turning to the specific theological premises of Judaism, another kind of diversity should be noted. Under the impact of the modern scientific mood, a divergence is developing within Judaism between naturalists and supernaturalists, between those who stress the immanence of God within nature and those who emphasize His transcendence above and beyond nature. This schism is to be found in both the Conservative and Reform movements. It has aroused much attention from Jewish theologians during past decades and will doubtlessly continue to do so.

With the diversities within Judaism understood, the function and role of theology clarified, the absence of a dogmatic creed recognized—what are the commonly accepted elements and emphases in our religious climate of conviction?

CHAPTER THREE

One and Only One

THE MOST IMPORTANT characteristic of Jewish religious belief is its uncompromising monotheism. Our faith is epitomized in its so-called watchword the *Shema*, repeated fervently during every morning and evening service of worship and recited by each observant Jew as the last conscious act of his life: "*Shema Yis-ra-ayl, Adonai Elohaynu, Adonai echad.*" It can be translated either as "Hear, O Israel, the Lord our God, the Lord is one," or "Hear, O Israel, the Eternal is our God, the Eternal alone." By either variant the *Shema* attests eloquently to the truth that for all religious Jews, God is one and unique.

It is alleged from time to time that we Jews were not the first people in history to hit upon the idea of one universal God, that the Egyptian Pharaoh Ikhnaton, for example, achieved the insight of monotheism before Moses did. His innovation, however, even if it actually occurred, was short-lived. There is no record of any large number of Egyptians agreeing with him, and after his death all Egypt reverted to the worship of many gods. Of equal importance is the fact that no ethical compulsions were associated with Ikhnaton's allegiance to Aton.

Only among Jews in antiquity was an entire people called upon to reject all gods and demigods in favor of the one universal God. And only among Jews was this one God

27

unalterably identified with the pursuit of righteousness. So rigidly did the Jewish people cling to monotheism that they were prohibited from entering a grove where an idol was located, even for the innocent purpose of being shaded from the sun, lest that act be misinterpreted by an observer or they be tempted to join in idolatrous worship.[1]

More important even than the uniqueness of Judaism as the originator of strict monotheism is its continued distinctiveness in this respect today. True, on a sophisticated, erudite level of thought it may be possible somehow to reconcile the Christian Trinity with the worship of a single God. But for vast multitudes of average Christians the emphasis on three Persons—the Father, the Son, and the Holy Ghost—contaminates pure monotheism with compromise and confusion. Even renowned Christian theologians have confessed that how God can simultaneously be One and Three is an impenetrable mystery. The dilemma of ordinary folk is even greater. In following Christian liturgy it is often extremely difficult to ascertain whether the prayers are addressed to God or Jesus or both, whether, indeed, the two are identical or distinct.

It is not too difficult to reconstruct how the problem probably arose. It had been Paul's hope that all Jews would follow him into the new faith based on the conviction that Jesus was the Christ. Very soon, however, it became apparent that few Jews were prepared to do so. If Christianity were to take root and spread, clearly it would have to appeal to the larger Roman world. The concept of a single, abstract, intangible God was far too difficult for most people to understand and accept. Hence there came about a grafting of Jewish monotheism and pagan polytheism with its man-gods who could be seen and heard. The Trinity inevitably resulted.

This fusion was and remains totally unacceptable to Jews, all Jews. For us, God is God and humans are human.

Though there be a bit of divinity within each of us, in
essence the human and the divine are not to be confused.
Our tradition tells us that the reason the burial place of
Moses is not identified in the Bible is precisely so that no
attempt could ever be made to idolize or divinize him. He
and all other spiritual geniuses of Judaism are described as
imperfect people, with manifest faults and flaws. The
ambivalence in Christianity between God and Christ is
utterly foreign to Judaism. We believe in one, unique God—
beyond comparison or full comprehension. Not without
good cause did Rabbi Abba Hillel Silver call the Jew "the
monitor of monotheism in the world."[2]

The Hebrew word *echad* carries a qualitative as well as a
quantitative connotation. It means *one;* it also means
unique. The *Shema,* quoted in the first paragraph of this
chapter, therefore reminds us that, unlike any other form
of existence or life known to us, God is purely spiritual. A
legend tells that after the Roman conquest of Jerusalem,
Pompey forced his way into the Holy of Holies, the inner
sanctum of the Temple, into which the high priest alone
was permitted to enter, and even he on the Day of Atonement (*Yom Kippur*) only. The purpose of the Roman
general was to ascertain the nature of this strange Jewish
God. All that he discovered, however, was an empty room!
To the Jew, such a discovery would not be disillusioning,
for God is beyond tabulation or measurement. "I will make
all My goodness pass before you . . . but you cannot see
My face, for man may not see Me and live" (Exodus 33:19).

The reference to God's face must be understood poetically. The Bible frequently speaks of God in human terms.
Its Jewish interpreters always realized, however, that such
language is figurative. We refer to God's face or voice or
hand in much the same way that we describe the shoulder
of a mountain or the mouth of a river. The *Shema* enjoins
us to remember that God is both one and unique. It is

imperative that this concept be clearly understood at the outset. Most of what follows is in a very real sense the issue of this first singular trait of Judaism.

If God is one and we are created in His image, we must also be one. Hence Judaism has never accepted a dichotomy, that is, a division, between body and soul. Judaism believes exclusive emphasis on either body or soul to be unrealistic and harmful. Paganism, both ancient and modern, conceives us as purely body, with physical pleasure to be courted and physical pain to be shunned. Christianity, in many of its manifestations, has viewed the physical part of human beings as something reprehensible, assigning almost exclusive emphasis to our spiritual identity.

Judaism sees us as an indivisible unity of the physical and the spiritual. It defines spirituality or the soul as the non-physical or trans-physical aspect of human life. Glands are physical; emotions and personality, both very much affected by glands, are spiritual. The brain is physical; mind and thought, both dependent upon the functioning of brain, are spiritual. One definition of soul is the capacity to create and appreciate truth, beauty, and moral goodness. Our souls function through our minds, our aesthetic sensitivities, and our consciences.

In its insistence that the physical and spiritual aspects of a person are phases of a single unit, Judaism has anticipated the findings of modern science. Today we know of a certainty that every illness is partly physical and partly emotional; each affects the other. When we suffer physical indigestion, our emotions are altered in consequence. When we are emotionally distressed, indigestion often results. Physicians have long known what Judaism discovered even earlier: the physical and non-physical components of human experience are inseparable.

A rabbinic parable attests to this. The story is told of a

blind man who carried a lame man into an orchard where together they stole some fruit. To the question of which was the guilty party, the rabbis answered: both—neither could have carried out the theft without the other. The two men represented the body and the soul. Together they constitute an indivisible unity.

Jews do not all agree on the origin of the soul. Some of us would subscribe to the Catholic theory that only our bodies have been produced through the evolutionary process, while our souls are a direct, supernatural gift from God. Most contemporary Jews, consistent with the unitary view upheld by both Judaism and science, would say instead that our souls too are products of evolution; they are the highest stage achieved thus far by the evolutionary process as it operates on our planet. The modern Jew would say that physical evolution had to reach a certain level of development before the spiritual could emerge from it. Only after the brain had developed a certain size and complexity was it possible for such a thing as mind or thought to appear in human forms of life.

Because Judaism holds a person to be a unified being, it has never looked upon his body as something inferior or contemptible. Some religions have. We are warned by our tradition never to dwell in a town that lacks either a bathhouse or a physician. We look upon medical skill as an adjunct to God's healing power and deem it to be sinful for a sick person to refuse medical aid. We see prayer as an important supplement to medicine in the healing process, not as a substitute for it. Once when Hillel bade his disciples farewell they asked where he was going. He answered, "To perform a religious duty." They asked which religious duty and he replied, "I am going to bathe." After they had expressed amazement at his designation of a bath as a religious duty, he explained, "If the statues of kings in public places are carefully scoured and washed to improve their appearance, how much more should I bathe my body, which is fashioned in the image of God."[3]

Similarly, Maimonides considered it a religious duty to take regular exercise for the maintenance of good health;[4] a sixteenth-century rabbi specifically permitted the playing of hand tennis on the Sabbath for this reason.[5]

The absence of dichotomy between body and soul and the great value assigned to the body explain why there has never been a major strain of asceticism in Judaism, as there has been in most faiths including Christianity. An ancient Jewish sage asserted: "He who sees a legitimate pleasure and does not avail himself of it is an ingrate against God who made it possible."[6] Another rabbi made bold to say that when we die we shall be called to account for every legitimate pleasure we have failed to enjoy.[7]

Except for an occasional minor sect of extremists, Judaism never prohibited such innocent pastimes as moderate dancing or reasonable playing of cards or temperate drinking. Only excesses were condemned. Judaism has never sponsored any major monastic movement. Many competent observers have credited the demonstrably superior sobriety of Jews, even in our own time, at least in part to the fact that the average Jewish child has been allowed to drink alcoholic beverages in his home, especially as he celebrated the Sabbath and holidays.

Nowhere is the absence of asceticism in Jewish life more impressive than in the fact that even our mystics were devoid of it. The mystics of all other religions have universally condemned physical pleasure. Israel Baal Shem Tov, founder of modern Jewish mysticism, warned: "He who does harm to his body, does harm to his soul."[8] Jewish mystics demonstrated wholesome acceptance of drink, of normal sex life, and of all the so-called pleasures of the flesh. For Judaism, because God is one, each of us, too, is one. Body and soul are pricelessly integrated aspects of our fundamental oneness.

Just as human unity reflects and attests to divine unity, so also in Jewish thought there is no rigid distinction between the sacred and the profane. Martin Buber put it very well when he said that for the Jew, life is divided not into the sacred versus the profane, but rather into the sacred and the not-yet-sacred. Even the remotest, most inaccessible corners of experience are susceptible to sanctification. The Jew faces an inescapable responsibility to make the most mundane moment holy.

This is why there is a Hebrew blessing to be recited by the observant Jew for just about everything he does. He is expected, in all, to voice one hundred benedictions a day:[9] when he retires at night and reawakens in the morning; on departing for a journey and returning from it safely; in the presence of thunder or when inspired by natural beauty. There is a Jewish formula for thanking God even when one uses the bathroom or anticipates sexual intercourse with his wife!

A chasidic disciple was once asked what the most important act in the world was for his master. He replied, "Whatever he happens to be doing at the moment." The Baal Shem Tov himself once commented on the verse, "All that your hand finds to do, do in your strength." As an example of the way in which faith can be translated into action, he said that a cobbler at his bench must sew together the upper leather and sole of the shoe in such manner that he will simultaneously be joining God and His *Shechinah*, His holy presence. We shall have more to say later about the meaning of holiness in Judaism. The important truth to be remembered now is that if each human being is one and life is one, holiness must pervade the whole, not be restricted to special compartments or occasions.

A full understanding of the *Shema* carries into our ethical strivings too. If God is one and we are one, a single code of ethics must apply to all of us in all situations. There cannot be one standard for the home, another for the factory or office, one for white and privileged folk, another for those of different-colored skin or inferior economic status. The way we live, moreover, must be consistent with our theological beliefs. Our tenets of faith may be premises which are reflected in deeds, or our patterns of behavior may constitute building blocks which support theological conclusions. Whichever is the case, or even if both are partially true, there must be a oneness, a wholeness, in what we profess and what we do. Our actions must be consonant with all the connotations of the *Shema* which have already been considered, as well as with certain additional theological presuppositions of Judaism.

Foremost among these is the profound conviction that our ethical ideals are more than just projections of human intelligence and will; they are part of the very structure and substance of the universe. Judaism recognizes two kinds of natural law: the physical, and the spiritual or moral. A classic example of the first is the law of gravity. We neither invented nor created it. It was a characteristic of the universe before any human being was on the scene to discover it. All else being equal, in the measure that we learn of it and try to conform to it, things will go well with us. If we foolishly ignore or defy it, the consequence will be catastrophe. In much the same way, Judaism proclaims, there is spiritual-moral law operative in the universe. Though not so immediately apparent nor so easily discovered as law of the physical variety it, too, is a trait of the universe which we must attempt to discover and to which we must conform if we would live happy and successful lives. Only those human laws and ideals which are consistent with the observable traits of our universe may be accepted as authentic or valid.

The relationship between physical and spiritual natural law was poignantly and impressively illustrated during the space flight of Apollo 8 in the waning days of 1968. The first astronauts to circle the moon succeeded because they were aware of all the physical laws governing their flight and had completely conformed to those laws. That they recognized the existence of spiritual law also became evident on Christmas Eve, when they read from outer space the opening verses of Genesis, describing how God created the universe.

A second emphasis of Jewish theology, intimately associated with ethics, is the high value it assigns to human nature. There is no doctrine of Original Sin in Judaism. After each day of Creation except one, we are told, God surveyed all that He had fashioned and declared it to be good. This refusal of our faith to brand us initially and innately evil is no starry-eyed romanticism, no blinking of reality. We hold that two impulses are components of our basic nature, an impulse toward good and an impulse toward evil. Each of us is the arbiter between them, endowed from birth with enough potential judgment and power to determine which will be victorious in his own life. Judaism does not permit its adherents to shift this responsibility to either the Devil or God.

Theologically, we see neither consistency nor sense in saying that we are created in God's image, then depicting us as if we were the devil incarnate. Psychologically, we believe it to be grossly unfair, even extremely damaging, to begin by challenging us to strive for a Christlike perfection, then to tell us that the attempt is in any event foredoomed to fail because we are blighted from birth by congenital contamination. It is not only more healthful but also more conducive to ethical effort to say, as our tradition does, that Adam was a normal human combination of the two impulses and that the whole human race descended from him "so that no sinner may say: 'I am a sinner by inheritance, being a descendant of sinners,' and no saint may say: 'I am a saint by virtue of my descent from saints.' "[10]

The very rare hints of something resembling Original Sin which were articulated from time to time by an isolated individual were firmly repudiated by sages in the mainstream of Jewish thought. The authentic view of our heritage is that of the Talmud, which says that before birth we are admonished: "Always bear in mind that the Holy One, praised be He, is pure, that His ministers are pure and that the soul which He gave you is pure; if you preserve it in purity, well and good, but if not, I will take it away from you."[11]

The notion of Original Sin has distressed many modern Christian theologians too. Accordingly, they have refined and reinterpreted it to mean not that we are irredeemably condemned from birth to ineradicable sin, but that we possess a natural tendency to err. This comes remarkably close to the Jewish concept of the impulse toward evil, without suggesting—as Judaism does—that we are also born with an innate tendency to do good. In Christianity, as in Judaism, much effort is being expended in our time to reinterpret ancient doctrines in the light of modern knowledge.

A third Jewish theological hypothesis is that humanity is God's partner in the ethical enterprise. One of the rabbis said explicitly, "Each person is a partner of the Holy One, praised be He." Another declared, "He who performs a moral act, as for instance, a judge who pronounces a moral judgment, associates himself with God in the creation of the world." Talmudic tradition tells us that at the instant of conception every external circumstance about a person is determined—whether he is to be tall or short, stout or lean, handsome or ugly, brilliant or dull. The one thing which is not so determined is whether he is to be righteous or wicked; this he must decide for himself.[12]

Our high estate in Jewish thought, as well as our inescapable ethical responsibility, derives especially from our partnership with God. The ancient rabbis were bold in proclaiming that God intentionally left His creation incomplete so that we could improve it. Thus the Talmud expounds: "Tineus Rufus asked Rabbi Akiba: 'Who makes more beautiful things, God or man?' Rabbi Akiba answered: 'Man makes more beautiful things . . .' He showed him ears of grain and cakes and said: 'The ears of grain are God's work, the cakes are man's. You see that man's works are more beautiful.' Then he brought him raw flax and some finished linen garments. He said to him: 'You see again that what man creates is more beautiful.' "[13]

Another authority cited in the Talmud pursued the same thought: "Whatever was created by God during the six days of Creation needs further improvement; for example, mustard needs sweetening, vetches need sweetening, wheat needs grinding. Even man is subject to improvement."[14]

In a mood of poetic fantasy an ancient rabbi pictured God about to give the Ten Commandments to Moses. Each had a hand on the tablets when God noticed that the Israelites were worshiping the molten calf Aaron had made for them. He was so infuriated that He began to withdraw the tablets, determined not to give them to the people after all. Whereupon, we are told, Moses exerted himself with a sudden burst of energy, pulling the Commandments, so to speak, out of the divine grasp.[15]

This was a bold way of expressing the thought that God alone cannot accomplish our ethical improvement. He makes it possible; only we can achieve it.

All religious Jews, at all times since Judaism began to assume its normative form, would agree with the theological opinions summarized to this point: that God, hence the universe and we too, are each unified and together constitute a unity; that the physical and the spiritual, the sacred and the mundane are one; that our ethics must inhere in and emerge from our estimate of the universe; that our values and ideals are projections from the nature of reality itself; that we are inherently good and are creative ethical partners of the Divine. Modern science has added certain overtones to these ancient insights. Though they may not be entirely understandable or acceptable to all contemporary Jews, they should be mentioned here, among other reasons because many Jewish thinkers are convinced they constitute the most probable and hopeful direction for further theological exploration.

Physicists, for example, tell us that the universe is indeed one in ways our ancestors could not even have suspected. Time and space are one; they are understood now as aspects of the same fundamental reality. Matter and energy are one: at the risk of oversimplification it may be said that matter is energy at rest; energy is matter in motion. Biologists add that the inorganic and the organic are one; they no longer think in terms of a complete separation of the lifeless from the living. The potential for life was present even before life itself first appeared; the viruses may well be a transition or bridge between the inorganic and the organic.

We now know—as our ancestors at best could only have suspected—that the same physical laws which govern the universe on its largest scale prevail also in its minutest dimensions. The identical chemical elements we have identified as components of our own bodies have been revealed by our most powerful radio telescopes to exist at the farthermost reaches of outer space. The movement of protons, electrons, and neutrons within an atom corresponds astonishingly to the movement of planets in a solar system around their sun. The arrangement of chromosomes within living cells is precisely the same in number and function in a celery stalk, a toad, and a human being.

The evidence is impressive and can be documented over and over again. The entire universe in its vast complexity is one ultimate basic reality; the Eternal, our God, really is one!

A distinguished British mathematician, Dr. J. Bronowski, may not have been aware of the fact that he was echoing and reinforcing the *Shema* when he said in a lecture at the Massachusetts Institute of Technology: "All science is the search for unity in hidden likenesses. . . . Science is nothing else than the search to discover unity in the wild variety of nature—or more exactly, in the variety of our experience."[16] Near the end of his life Dr. Albert Einstein was engaged in a quest for one formula which would embrace and express the totality of all existence. He too was reaffirming in a more precise and prosaic way the truth which Judaism has sought to express poetically in its repetition of the *Shema*.

The confluence of modern scientific insight with ancient Jewish teaching has been noted by many competent observers, among them Dr. Ralph W. Burhoe: "The scientific faith that all things are variants in a single system, that one law rules the cosmos from end to end, from the biggest to the littlest, is a faith that grows stronger with each succeeding new discovery that shows the relationship between phenomena that previously did not seem to be related. Today this faith is so high that we have little doubt but that there is a continuity from man to amoeba to molecule. There is no separation of man from his origin or from his fellow men. We are indeed all brothers. . . ."[17]

Science also supplements our earlier assertion that nature can provide us with ethical guidelines. Some students of the subject are convinced that evolution is entirely the result of chance mutations and natural selection, a process which possesses no meaningful direction. Others, however, perceive in it direction of the most significant sort. Elsewhere* I have developed at some length the directions one can discern in evolution. They are, briefly, trends toward organization and order, toward cooperation in contrast to competition, toward uniqueness and individuality, toward increased freedom and toward enlarged spirituality. Prior to the appearance of humanity, these constituted the automatic thrusts of the evolutionary process. From the human point forward, they are no longer automatic. There will be further movement in these directions only if we are aware of the possibilities and so act that they can be realized. In modern, scientifically oriented terms, this is what it means to proclaim that we are partners in God's creative work.

On its surface, the *Shema* is a simple statement, yet the Jew who pronounces it is asserting more than he may realize—about God, the universe, life, himself. He has come close to summarizing the very heart of Jewish religious belief.

* *Man's Best Hope* (New York Random House, 1961), Ch. 4.

Wings of the Morning (New York: Union of American Hebrew Congregations 1969), Ch. 5.

CHAPTER FOUR

Contrasts

WE HAVE ALREADY SEEN a sharp distinction between
Judaism and Christianity regarding human nature. However liberally or poetically interpreted, the doctrine of Original Sin poses a gulf between the two faiths.
There are other noteworthy differences too. The new ecumenical mood, so auspiciously inaugurated by Pope John
XXIII, has helped ameliorate the strained relations between Judaism and Christianity. One of its less fortunate
consequences, however, has been the implication that all
faiths are substantially similar, that they constitute only
minor variations of a single theme; this conclusion is not
true. There is much common ground shared by Judaism
and Christianity, but we do massive injustice to both traditions when we lightly gloss over the very real divergences
in their views. In continuing our quest for an accurate
understanding of Jewish theology, let us inquire further
into these disagreements.

The most crucial difference of all is with reference to
the person and importance of Jesus. To most Christians
he is the Christ, the miraculously produced and miracle-
producing messiah, dispatched by God for the redemption
of sinners. Though Jews may differ among themselves in
their attitudes toward Jesus, no Jew can accept him as
messiah.

Ancient Jewish prophecy, to be sure, anticipated the coming of a messiah, a scion of the House of David, who would usher in what is generally referred to in secular terms as utopia. His coming would mark the end of war, poverty, disease, injustice, and all the other oppressive burdens which blight the human lot. In ancient Judaism, however, the person of the messiah was never so significant as the consequences of his coming. Nor was he in any respect ever confused with God Himself. He was to be God's messenger, not His alter ego—His delegate, not His substitute. In my World War II experience as a Marine Corps chaplain I met Christians who were astonished to learn that Jews believe in God. They had themselves so confused the identities of God and Christ that it was difficult for them to reconcile the retention of the first, the Deity, with the rejection of the second, Jesus as the messiah. There could be no such obscurity in Judaism.

In the long course of Jewish history Jesus was only one of several men who either professed themselves to be the messiah, or on whose behalf such claims were advanced by followers. Each in turn had his loyal disciples, but none was ever universally accepted or acclaimed. The test of an alleged messiah was whether he succeeded in initiating the new social and historical conditions he was supposed to bring. In Jewish doctrine the messianic age was to occur as the culmination of history. So long as Jews were still persecuted, wars still waged, injustice still perpetrated, the alleged messiah was rejected as a pretender, albeit perhaps a sincere and persuaded one. Judaism never managed to adjust its original messianic expectation by promulgating a doctrine of the Second Coming. The true messiah would not need another chance.

What, then, does Jesus represent to the Jew? The answers will vary. It would be dishonest to deny that because of the inhuman persecutions inflicted on our people through

the centuries by ostensible Christians, cruelties and pun-
ishments often condoned by the Church itself, to some
Jews the very name of Jesus remains anathema. My father
was born in a small Russo-Lithuanian town where he spent
his childhood and adolescence. Coming to this country in
his late teens, he studied medicine and became physician
to many families, Christian as well as Jewish. He was a
kindly, gentle, liberal, moderate man who seldom expressed hostility to anyone. Yet I recall his saying, even in
his advanced years, that because of the pogroms he witnessed as a young child—pogroms usually emanating from
the local church at Christmas or Easter time—he was never
able to pass a church structure and see the cross on it without feeling chills traversing his spine.

Such visceral reactions are not to be lightly dismissed.
Most of us Jews, however, especially those who were born
in the United States and have lived our entire lives here, do
not feel this way about Jesus.

In our view Jesus was born a Jew, lived as a Jew, died a
Jew. We do not believe he had any intention of establishing
a new faith. We recognize him to have been a superb
teacher of Judaism. Nearly all the content of his teaching
had been anticipated by the biblical prophets from six to
eight centuries before his time. Even his method of teaching by parable was characteristic of ancient Jewish pedagogy. He was a critic of much in Judaism that warranted
criticism in his time, following the precedent of Moses,
Amos, Isaiah, Jeremiah, and innumerable other Jews. We
see Judaism as the religion *of* Jesus, Christianity as a religion *about* Jesus. We believe that if he returned to earth
now, he would be much more comfortable in a synagogue
than a church. We Jews do not agree that any person can
be called the son or daughter of God more than any other.

Am I distorting history or indulging in special pleading
when I assert that Jesus was a Jew? By no means! No less

an authority than Julius Wellhausen, dean of all early Christian Bible scholars, father of "Higher Criticism" of the Bible, in some respect an anti-Semite, was forced by his studies to conclude: "Jesus was not a Christian; he was a Jew. He did not preach a new faith, but taught men to do the will of God; and in his opinion, as also in that of the Jews, the will of God was to be found in the Law of Moses and in the other books of Scripture."

Is it possible to be both a Jew and a Christian at the same time? Karl M.* and his companions in "Jews for Jesus" would say yes. Indeed, the official franchise of their group reads: "We are a group of people who have come to believe that Jesus is the Messiah of Israel. We believe that the New Testament and the Old Testament are true. We believe in one true God and that the Godhead is fully revealed in the person of Jesus Christ. Furthermore, we believe that the God of Abraham, Isaac, and Jacob is the One who made us Jews. Hence, we are 'Jews for Jesus.' "

Is it true that one can accept Jesus, yet remain a Jew? Yes . . . and no. I can accept Jesus as an exemplary human being, not as part of the Godhead. I accept and respect him as a skilled and eloquent teacher of Judaism, not as the Christ. I accept him as a restless rebel against hypocrisy, as a compassionate counselor, as one who stressed the spirit over the letter of the law, though he knew the letter to be important too. But the instant I accept Jesus as the messiah, I relinquish my legitimate claim to be a Jew.

There is an ambivalence on this point in ancient and medieval Jewish law. According to rabbinic authorities, one who is born of Jewish parents or—in the case of parents whose religious affiliations differ—of a Jewish mother remains a Jew all his life. He may, to be sure, be a deficient

* See p. 7.

or inadequate Jew; but regardless of anything he does or fails to do, he is still legally Jewish. Still, in the eyes of the populace and of some among the rabbis, accepting Jesus as the messiah was deemed an act of apostasy which removed one from Judaism. If such a person relented later and wished to be considered a Jew again, no conversion process was required. But so long as he professed to believe in Jesus as the Christ, he was not thought of as a Jew.

In a way, members of "Jews for Jesus" are living in the wrong century. They were born nineteen hundred years too late and are waging a battle which was fought and lost nearly two millennia ago. The very first followers of Jesus, the disciples and those who came immediately after them, were Jews who believed Jesus to be the messiah. They tried their best to convince all Jews that this was so. They failed. The overwhelming majority of their fellow Jews, then and ever since, remain unconvinced.

Karl. M. would have a ready answer to our scepticism. He would turn triumphantly to Isaiah and his predictions about the messiah. One by one he would list Isaiah's prophecies, one by one elaborate how everything the earlier leader had foretold was true of Jesus. Did this not prove that Jesus was in fact the messiah, that Jews are obdurately misguided in refusing to accept him as such?

It proves no such thing. What is frequently forgotten is that the Gospels, in which all these putative facts about Jesus are so painstakingly recorded, were by their own testimony written in the service of a message. They were written a generation after the death of Jesus by men whose precise purpose it was to establish that Jesus was the messiah foretold by Isaiah.

Is this only the self-serving judgment of a Jew? Not at all. It has been accepted by an increasing number of scientifically reputable Christian scholars of the New Testament. One of the most eminent of them, Rudolf Bultmann, has written: "We conclude that the whole framework of the history of Jesus must be viewed as an editorial construction, and that therewith a whole series of typical scenes which, because of their ecclesiastical use and their poetic and artistic associations, we had looked upon as scenes in the life of Jesus, must be viewed as creations of the evangelists."

We Jews do not quarrel with Christians over their conviction that Jesus was the divinely dispatched messiah. We respect them and their beliefs. Our quarrel is twofold: with the notion that accepting Jesus as the Christ is the culmination of Judaism; and with the assertion that it is possible, for one individual at one and the same time, to be both Christian and Jewish. By deluding themselves into supposing this to be a tenable option, "Jews for Jesus" risk being neither Jewish nor Christian.

What do Jews believe about the messiah? Most Orthodox Jews harbor the same expectations and hopes as their biblical ancestors. The difference between them and Christians is largely one of identity and timing. They still await him who, Christians believe, has already come, but they do not expect the messiah to be the Son of God. Most non-Orthodox Jews hinge their hopes more on the messianic age than on an individual messiah. To them the latter symbolizes the enduring possibility of improvement in human affairs, the potential within us and our universe to transform wickedness and evil into goodness by cooperating with God. Many, if not most, modern Jews would subscribe to the underlying spirit of a chasidic tale concerning a disciple who asked his master when the messiah would come. The questioner was perturbed when he heard by way of reply that his rabbi did not expect the messiah at all. This startling answer was then explained: There is a spark of messiah in each of us; when we succeed in putting together all our individual messianic sparks, the result will constitute the coming of the messiah!

Another stark divergence between Judaism and Christianity is the absence in our faith of anything like a doctrine of vicarious atonement. All branches and interpretations of the Jewish religion hold that atonement can be obtained only by the individual sinner himself—by deed, not merely by intention or word. We are taught that even the most sacred occasion of the year, the Day of Atonement (*Yom Kippur*), helps us to atone only for the sins we have committed against God. The sins we have perpetrated against other human beings will not be forgiven until we have made reparation for any damages we may have caused them. There is a precious tradition among us—unfortunately no longer commonly practiced—that anyone who feels an injustice has been done him by another member of the congregation may interrupt the religious service on *Yom Kippur* to demand restitution. The service may not continue until his claim is adjudicated.

No matter how pious or fervent his declaration of atonement, one is not fully forgiven until he successfully resists the opportunity to commit the same sin under the same circumstances. According to the teachings of Judaism, no one else—neither God nor human—can achieve atonement for me. I cannot attain it even for myself except by scrupulous correction of whatever I may have done wrong, and by refraining from committing the same sin again.

The Talmud leaves no room for misunderstanding or doubt: "If one is guilty of sin and confesses it and does not change his way, what is he like? He is like a person who holds a defiling object in his hand even while he immerses himself in purifying waters. All the waters in the world will not avail him. He remains unclean because he clings to his defilement."

Closely related to the foregoing is the matter of salvation, a theological concept which never assumed in Judaism anything remotely resembling its importance to Christianty. If we are not foredoomed to sin and guilt by heredity, there is nothing from which we need to be saved. To the degree that a belief in salvation functioned in Jewish thought, it was more closely allied to truly human fulfillment than to being saved from a condition of primordial disgrace. One of the Hebrew words for sin is *chatah*, the same verb used for missing the mark when shooting at a target. We are meant to realize the divine potential within us. We miss the mark when we fail to do so. We attain salvation when we achieve our full spiritual potential as human beings, created in the image of God. In the perspective of Judaism, when I create and appreciate the maximum of truth, beauty, and goodness within my capacities, I am "saved."

One cannot successfully discuss Jewish theology without paying some attention to the question of whether we Jews look upon ourselves as a chosen people. In the past we certainly have. Biblical tradition describes a covenant between our people and God, an agreement initially established in the days of Abraham: "When Abram was ninety-nine years old, the Lord appeared to Abram and said to him, 'Walk in My ways and be blameless. I will establish My covenant between Me and you, and I will make you exceedingly numerous. . . . I will maintain my covenant between Me and you, and your offspring to come, as an everlasting covenant throughout the ages, to be God to you and to your offspring to come. I will give the land you sojourn in to you and your offspring to come, all the land of Canaan, as an everlasting possession. I will be their God. . . . As for you, you shall keep My covenant, you and your offspring to come, throughout the ages.' "

The concept of covenant is immensely important in Jewish thought and faith. The very ceremony through which a Jewish boy has for centuries been initiated into the community on the eighth day after his birth is called *breet meelah*, the *covenant* of circumcision.* Conservative and Reform Jews are now developing parallel rituals for admitting a girl child, too, into the covenant which God established between himself and Abraham's descendants.

One misses the point inexcusably in failing to observe that this covenant was a two-way contract. It imposed stringent obligations on the Jewish people: only if they kept their part of the bargain was God obliged to fulfill His. The covenant was conditional.

This is reiterated innumerable times in scripture. "If you will obey My voice and keep My covenant, then you shall be My own treasure from among all peoples, for all the earth is Mine; and you shall be unto Me a kingdom of priests and a holy nation." Always an *if*! Always a burden of responsibility from which this people could never escape!

No one understood or expressed the nature of that responsibility better than the prophet Isaiah:

He shall make righteousness go forth to the nations . . .
He will not fail, or be discouraged
Until he has established justice throughout the
world . . .

Many Christian spokesmen have misconstrued this and similar verses as describing the messiah. Jewish scholars, who are much closer to the language and spirit of the original, have never doubted these words were descriptive of the entire Jewish people.

Post-biblical authorities were no less careful in reminding Jews that if they had indeed been chosen, it was for additional responsibilities, not for special privilege. A Midrash (early

* See p. 155.

medieval sermonic comment on a biblical text) quotes God as saying to our ancestors: "Had it not been for your acceptance of My Torah, I would not have given you any special recognition, nor would I have treated you any better than idolaters."[1]

Just what being chosen meant in Jewish tradition is beautifully enunciated in a prayer from the Talmud, which is supposed to be recited by every Jew as he departs from the House of Study: "I give thanks before Thee, O Lord my God and God of my fathers, that Thou hast set my lot among those who sit in the House of Study and the Synagogue, and hast not set my lot with those who frequent the theaters and circuses; for while I labor to inherit Paradise, they labor for the pit of destruction."

The Midrash leaves no room for doubt that to be chosen means to assume extraordinary obligation, not to benefit from special privilege. The point of the following parable will be self-evident: "A priest married two wives, one a priest's daughter and the other a lay-Israelite's daughter. He handed to them flour for an offering, which they defiled, and each blamed the other for it. What did the priest do? He ignored the wife who was a layman's daughter and began to chide the priest's daughter. She said to him, 'My lord, why do you ignore the other and rebuke me?' He answered, 'She is the daughter of a layman and was not taught in her father's house the sanctity of the flour for an offering; but you are a priest's daughter, and you were taught this in your father's house. That is why I overlook her and reprimand you.' "

Is the doctrine of the chosen people borne out by history? An honest appraisal of reality will disclose that the Jewish people has in fact demonstrated a unique religious genius. Every civilization, like each individual, can be said to offer its own kind of contribution to the sum total of human welfare. The ancient Greeks exhibited a special bent for creativity in the visual arts, the Romans in the field of law. We in the United States have displayed extraordinary national ability in the direction of democracy. The Jew, more than any other people, has shown an exceptional capacity to inquire into the cosmic meaning of the human experience and to distill from that meaning a code of ethical standards by which we can become most truly human.

With or without the theological doctrine of a chosen people, it is historical fact that, when other peoples were still worshiping a multiplicity of gods, the Jew first glimpsed a single Ultimate Reality. While others yet conceived their deities as enlarged supermen, the Jew thought of God as purely spiritual. When others contemplated their religious responsibilities primarily in terms of ritual, the Jew assigned primacy to ethics. Even before science had commenced to supply factual reinforcement, the Jew had surmised intuitively that the universe is characterized by oneness. It is no coincidence that, to this very day, every movement to enlarge the freedom of men and women attracts a disproportionate number of Jews. Later we shall observe this in detail. Meanwhile, any sober reading of history confirms the fact that there has been something unique about the Jewish people.

Both Christians and Jews have recognized this to be true. Leo Tolstoy, Russian author and Christian mystic, wrote, "The Jew is that sacred being who has brought down from heaven the everlasting fire, and has illumined with it the entire world. He is the religious source, spring and fountain out of which all the rest of the peoples have drawn their beliefs and their religions." The late rabbi, Abraham Joshua Heschel, expressed himself this way: "We are God's stake in human history. We are the dawn and the dusk, the challenge and the test. How strange to be a Jew and to go astray on God's perilous errands."[2]

The Jewish concept of a chosen people involves a two-way relationship. Like the original covenant with Abraham, it remains operative only if the recipient upholds his part of the bargain. The idea of God's choosing the Jewish people is meaningful only if it implies that the Jewish people also choose God. Even in antiquity there were those who understood this. Though the rabbinic text proceeds to repudiate the notion, it quotes the following as the opinion of at least some Jews centuries ago: "We do not know whether the Lord chose Israel as His treasure or whether Israel chose the Holy One, blessed be He."[3]

It is a gross misreading of history to equate the Jewish doctrine of being chosen with such a noxious notion as the Nazi philosophy of a "master race." Two Jews—one ancient, the other modern—have captured most expressively the true meaning of being chosen as applied to their people. The prophet Amos imagined God's saying: "You only have I known of all the families of the earth; therefore will I visit upon you all your iniquities." A modern German-Jewish poet, Richard Beer-Hofmann, has perceptively written in his play *Jacob's Dream*:

> This is what "chosen" means:
> Not to know dreamless sleep,
> Visions at night—and voices round by day!
> Am I then chosen? Chosen that all suffering
> Calls me, demands me, and complains to me?
> That even the dumb look of the dying beast
> Asks me: "Why so?"

The modern religious Jew sees himself bound on two levels by a covenant with God: as an individual, and as part of a perennial people. He persists in remaining a Jew not merely out of stubbornness or pride, but because he is convinced that Jews—both personally and collectively—have special purposes to fulfill in the cosmic scheme of things. They must be more aware than others of the Spiritual Core which permeates all reality, more determined than others to develop the spiritual potential within themselves, more sensitive than others to the pain of the human condition which it is their responsibility to assuage.

Any people can be chosen. The prerequisite is to discover what it is especially qualified to accomplish for the spiritual enrichment of the whole human race, then to act on that discovery. The Jewish people in times past was entitled to consider itself chosen because in fact it did precisely this. Jews will continue to enjoy this privilege only so long as they deserve it.

It would be an incalculable tragedy if we Jews, who successfully preserved and developed our uniqueness through so many centuries of persecution and oppression, were now to surrender it in a time of freedom. Very often in history the price of equality for a minority group has been total acculturation, which means to say, becoming in every respect like the majority. There is grave danger now that instead of raising others to our level of cosmic inquiry and ethical compulsion, we Jews may bridge the gulf by accepting lower standards ourselves. This would be no less a pity and waste for history than for ourselves. It would drain all meaning from our doctrine of being a chosen people.

How does the Eternal reveal itself to humankind? Jewish tradition would respond: in a multiplicity of ways, both natural and supernatural. It would include in the category of revelation that which comes to a person "when I behold Thy heavens, the work of Thy fingers, the moon and the stars, which Thou hast established." A much higher degree of significance, however, would have been assigned by Jews of former times to revelation of a supernatural mode: to Moses ascending the peak of Sinai midst roaring thunder and flashing lightning, there to hear—perhaps quite literally—the words of the Ten Commandments

and of Torah, enunciated in the divine voice. Or to Jeremiah, thrashing about in the desperate attempt to renege
on his prophetic responsibility, hearing from on high the
words of challenge from which no escape was possible.

Yet there have always been some Jewish leaders, even
in days long past, who considered such passages and
descriptions as these to be poetic representations of the
natural rather than the supernatural. The number who so
interpret them has undeniably increased in this century.
Today significant numbers of rabbis—even if not a majority
—would say that whenever or wherever a human being,
touched by the creative Spiritual Core of reality, rises to a
new height in the creation or appreciation of truth, beauty,
or moral goodness, there and then revelation has occurred
again. The scientist in his laboratory, the composer at his
keyboard, the artist before his canvas—these may be just
as responsive to divine revelation as the preacher at his
pulpit or desk. However the word *revelation* be understood, faith in God can have little meaning or use unless
there are ways for the Divine to communicate with the
human. Such contact, in whatever way it be conceived, is
revelation.

The converse, our method of communicating with God,
is prayer. Here too we must expect wide variation among
Jews. Some believe, as did the bulk of their ancestors,
that every word we speak in prayer is audible to a divine
ear. Some may even think it possible by prayer to alter
the divine intention, though this was seldom supposed by
the wisest among their ancestors. And others—again, the
naturalists, shall we say the theological radicals?—hold
prayer to be any variety of reading, thinking, or medi-
tating which reinforces our relationship with the Highest,
which reminds us of our priceless heritage and ultimate
purpose, thereby stimulating us to reach out of what we
have been toward that which we can become. Jewish re-

ligious naturalists might define prayer as any intellectual, emotional, or aesthetic experience which seeks or strengthens their spiritual relationship to the universe. To them, prayer is analogous to reminding oneself on a journey of what the final destination is, of why it is important to reach it, of the best methods and routes to get there, of the resources available to assist one toward success. The Jewish religious naturalist does not expect prayer in any way to change God, but rather—by activating the God within himself, an aspect of God at large outside himself—to make possible a kind of conduct and a degree of spiritual realization which would otherwise have been beyond reach.

There is room within Judaism for both supernaturalistic and naturalistic interpretations of revelation and prayer. Their resemblance is more significant than their disparity. In both cases the believing Jew is confident that, within the universe and his own life, there exists a spiritual essence with which it is possible to establish two-way communication and through which his earthly career can be immensely elevated and enriched.

Jews have been no less vulnerable than others to the inroads of modernism on the practice of prayer. Several studies suggest that a lower proportion of Jews than of either Catholics or Protestants attends public worship services regularly. This may be due to numerous causes: the fact that Judaism is at least as much home- as synagogue-centered; the ignorance of so many Jews concerning the historic differences between prayer in their faith and prayer as conceived by others; our failure to reinterpret religion generally and prayer specifically in the light of today's scientific knowledge. Whatever the causes, there is an alarming gap between the teachings of Judaism and the practices of many contemporary Jews. This gap is among the most pressing challenges confronting Jewish religious leadership.

Does the religious Jew believe in miracles? The answer
has in part been suggested by our comments on revelation
and prayer. Some unquestionably do. They conceive God
to be unlimited in power, able to accomplish anything and
everything, to break even the apparently inviolate laws of
His own creation if He so desires. Others say that God
could break these natural laws if He wanted to, but chooses
forever not to do so. Still others have faith in God precisely
because His universe appears to be one of unvarying order;
they deny, therefore, even the theoretical possibility that
miracles could break through that order. They see God
especially in His promise to Noah:

> So long as the earth endures,
> Seedtime and harvest,
> Cold and heat,
> Summer and winter,
> Day and night,
> Shall not cease.

The problem of miracles bothered even some of the
medieval commentators and scholars. Maimonides, for
example, tried to have it both ways by suggesting that
the miracles recorded in scripture were built into the original plan of creation, so that they did not constitute exceptions. Once they had been implemented, however, no
further miracles were possible. If miracles be interpreted
to mean phenomena and events which are beyond our
capacity to comprehend, then indeed all religious Jews believe in miracles. But in the more ordinary understanding
of the word, there will be open and honest differences
within our ranks.

There is, finally, the issue of immortality. Faith in a life
after earthly death played a much smaller role in early
Judaism than in most faiths. Indeed, the Hebrew Bible
contains no such substantive doctrine at all. For every

scriptural passage proclaiming the possibility of life beyond the grave, another can be found which denies it. Both biblical attitudes are included in the book of Job. In one passage the book's protagonist says:

> But as for me, I know that my Redeemer liveth,
> And that he will witness at the last upon the dust;
> And when after this, my skin is destroyed,
> Then without my flesh shall I see God;
> Whom I, even I, shall see for myself,
> And mine eyes shall behold, and not another's.

That would seem to be about as unequivocal as anything could be. Yet the same Job says elsewhere:

> For there is hope of a tree,
> If it be cut down, that it will sprout again,
> And that the tender branch thereof will not cease.
> Though the root thereof wax old in the earth,
> And the stock thereof die in the ground;
> Yet through the scent of water it will bud,
> And put forth boughs like a plant.

> But man dieth, and lieth low;
> Yea, man perisheth, and where is he?
> As the waters fail from the sea,
> And the river is drained dry;
> So man lieth down and riseth not;
> Till the heavens be no more, they shall not awake,
> Nor be roused out of their sleep.

It was only in post-biblical Judaism that a doctrine of immortality became assertive and important.

Two factors conspired to effect this change. First, Jews came into sustained contact with other religions, particularly Persian Zoroastrianism, which had already developed concepts of immortality. Second, the Jewish people became exposed to terrible burdens of oppression and frustration. Deprived of fulfillment during their limited years on earth, anxious and frightened by the apparent success of the wicked while the righteous were suffering, they found it increasingly tempting to accept the faith of other groups that the injustices and dissatisfactions of this life would be compensated for in another life. In talmudic and medieval Judaism, therefore, much was said and believed about immortality.

There was never total agreement, however; the gamut of interpretation ranged all the way from physical resurrection to a purely spiritual extension of life beyond its earthly termination. Once again, essential Jewish faith can be summarized in a sentence: The religious Jew is confident that whatever is most important about his life on this planet will survive his physical death. This allows for wide latitudes of conceiving just what are the most significant aspects of this life and how they are believed to endure beyond the grave.

Inconsistencies often appeared not only among Jews but within the thought and faith structure of an individual Jew. In his personal creed, for example, Maimonides included resurrection of the dead. Yet in his major philosophical work resurrection is not mentioned. He also proposed a kind of selective immortality, reserving it for the righteous. The wicked, he said, are really dead while their hearts still pulse; how, then, could they be judged alive after death?

No discussion on the attitude of Judaism toward immortality can be concluded without reference to the predominant emphasis of our faith on life rather than death. The Talmud goes so far as to say that if a funeral procession and a bridal procession happen to reach an intersection simultaneously, the bride and her party go first. Our tradition sees both life and death as manifestations of the divine. Almost every Jewish funeral service includes the proclamation of Job: "The Eternal has given; the Eternal has taken away; praised be the name of the Eternal." Our liturgy contains an impressive prayer called the *Kad-*

dish, the Sanctification, which is recited in memory of those who have died. Perhaps the most amazing thing about the *Kaddish* in the form most commonly used is that it contains not a single word referring to death or the dead! It is a magnificent doxology in praise of God. Some of its sentiments and even its phrases are echoed in the Lord's Prayer of Christianity. Indeed, these hallowed Jewish words may have been the model for the prayer of Jesus. The *Kaddish* symbolizes and vocalizes the emphasis of Judaism that, even in our moments of deepest mourning and grief, we must be gratefully aware of God as the source of all existence and must reiterate our determination so to live that our years and those of our departed loved ones will acquire ultimate significance.

There is much more concern in Judaism for the right way to spend our span of earthly life than for what happens to us after it ends. On this point, as on so many others, Maimonides spoke in the accents of authentic Judaism:

> People complain that life is too short, that man's life ends before he is done preparing himself for it. The truth is that while our life is short, we live as though we had eternity at our disposal; we waste too much of life. Our lifetime, if we used it properly, is sufficient to accomplish the greatest of achievements. But if we squander our life, we feel as though our years are flying by too quickly, as though we have no time to achieve anything.
>
> The problem is not that we are allotted a short life, but rather that we are extravagant in spending it. Thus, a careless heir will quickly dissipate a huge estate; while a meagre inheritance will flourish in the hands of a wise and thrifty person. Of what, then, might we justly complain? That we live as if our life would last forever and do not wisely use the lifetime that is amply allotted to us.

Underlying the variations in their views of immortality is the common belief among Jews that our individual lives acquire their lasting significance from the larger context of which they form a part. Each person's life fits into everything which preceded it and everything that will follow it. It is meant to serve important purposes. The life of the individual who contributes to the fulfillment of these purposes never ends. Some Jews will interpret its continuance in identifiably personal terms. Others will say that the individual lives on in the memory of those who continue to cherish him, in the good he has accomplished, in his children, in whatever he has done to promote and advance the divine plan of the universe—which means to say, the further development of evolution toward nobler and loftier spiritual ends.

Judaism sees each individual life as a page in a book. However instructive or inspiring the content of a single page may be, it assumes its greatest significance only as it relates to that which precedes and follows it, to the total plan of which it forms a part. Our faith perspective sees that total plan as God's. Each of us has much to say in writing his own page. He achieves immortality in the measure that he contributes to the total context, consummating that which others have previously written, preparing the way for authors yet to come.

Here, then, in broad outline, is what the Jew believes: That a unitary cosmos, a unitary human race, and a unitary individual all reflect a single and singular God. That the physical and the spiritual, the sacred and the profane, are all one. That no area of human experience can be exempted from the nagging voice of conscience. That for the further implementation of His cosmic plan, God needs us as much as we need Him. That the covenant between Jews and their God imposes upon every one of us an extraordinarily high order of moral responsibility. That we can be godly but not God. That no one else can atone for my sins, and even I can do so only through improved deeds. That I can be both the receiver and the transmitter of communication between God and myself. That my life is more than a momentary aberration or accident; whatever it reflects of the divine will endure beyond my three score years and ten.

In a strangely significant way, even many secularist Jews today would subscribe to much in this complex of Jewish belief. Their vocabulary, to be sure, would differ. But our chapters thus far would come very close to articulating what they, too, believe about the universe and our place in it. To their own surprise—perhaps in some few cases even discomfort—the climate of conviction would still be essentially Jewish.

Our concentration on contrasts must not be allowed to blind us to the fact that Jews and Christians share much in common. At a time of crass materialism, both persuasions proclaim that spiritual goals should assume priority in any hierarchy of human values. Both assert that our life achieves its highest significance as part of a cosmic plan. Both impose moral obligations on their adherents. The differences should spur Christians as well as Jews to appreciate and refine their own traditions, not to assume postures of arrogant superiority toward each other. While appreciating our own uniqueness and respecting the other's, we need combined effort if the values we share are to be rendered effective.

CHAPTER FIVE

Correcting the Record

No PEOPLE IN HISTORY has been so persistently maligned as
the Jews. Later we shall find it necessary to refer briefly
to the physical persecutions inflicted upon them. Here our
concern is primarily with calloused, at times even libelous,
misrepresentation of Jewish doctrine. Not that the two
can be entirely separated. There is a theology of anti-
Semitism, without which the brutality of such groups as
the Nazis would have been improbable, perhaps impossible. It would be irresponsible to close our consideration
of Jewish belief without attending to the record and cor-
recting it.

We know why so many malicious errors about Judaism
and the Jewish people have been perpetuated. Reference
has already been made to the dilution of Jewish monotheism by Christianity in order to make the new faith palatable
to the pagan world. Something of the same motivation
enters into the origins of Christian theological anti-Semitism.
If—as we have surmised, as more than a few historians
agree, and as Jesus' very words, quoted by his followers,
attest—it was not the intention of Jesus to abandon Judaism or initiate a new religion, if he sought only to reform
and improve the Judaism he had inherited, then some jus-
tification had to be found by those who founded the new
faith in his name. Failings and flaws of major proportion

had to be identified in the old religion; otherwise, why was it necessary to take so drastic a step as to reject it?

Until very recently the assumption among Christians of greatest good will toward Jews has been that anti-Semitism is an aberration of Christianity, not indigenous to it. Only by misunderstanding the Christian message, it was supposed, could one sink to the level of anti-Semitic prejudice. This premise has been implicit in the several protestations against anti-Jewish prejudice issued by recent Popes as well as in the pronouncements of Vatican II. The ugly truth is only now beginning to dawn in the minds of a few Christian theologians that this is too easy an answer, that in fact there is much in Christian doctrine itself which is conducive toward anti-Semitism. Dr. A. Roy Eckardt, Protestant editor and teacher, has addressed himself to this issue:

> All the learned exegesis in the world cannot negate the truth that there are elements not only of anti-Judaism but of anti-Semitism in the New Testament. . . . We do not appear to realize—perhaps we do not wish to know—that until the church admits unqualifiedly, and goes out of its way to proclaim to the world, the anti-Semitic proclivities within sections of its basic canon, hostility to Jews will not finally be rooted out anywhere in Christian teaching.[1]

What are some of the specific traits of Christian theology which predispose the believer toward prejudice against Judaism? To begin with, the very designation of the Hebrew Bible as the Old Testament, especially in contrast to the immediate labeling of the Christian supplement to it as the New Testament. Except to a very limited proportion of the population, the word *old* in general implies inferiority vis-à-vis the *new*. Old people are less vigorous than young, old fashions in clothing less desirable than new, old cars less attractive than more recent models. These terms are even more harmful when used in a theological context. "Old Testament" suggests that there must have been something inferior and incomplete about it which required improvement by superimposition of a New Testament.

This is in fact exactly what Christianity has taught. That the old covenant between God and the Jewish people has been replaced by a new covenant between God and Christians. If the titles assigned by Christianity to the two sections of its scripture mean anything, they mean precisely that. Dr. Rosemary Ruether, a Roman Catholic visiting Lecturer at Howard University, has summed the matter up with accuracy: "Built into the treatment of the Jewish and Christian Bibles as Old and New Testaments respectively is the idea of Judaism as a superseded and obsolete religion, superseded not simply historically but theologically, superseded in terms of the covenant of God with Israel itself."[2]

A Christian religious educator in England, Ronald Goldman, pleading that children's horizons be broadened, betrays his professed liberalism by referring to the faith of the Hebrew Bible as "the primitive materialistic religion of the early Hebrews." He brands the exalted deity conceived by Moses "a nature god of storm and violence." Telling Christians how to teach the Bible, he advises:

> Unless some firm ideas are formed of what Jesus means for the world and what is the message of the New Testament, much of the Old Testament may be taken on its face value. Instead, the New Testament must be used as a yardstick by which the value of the Old can be measured. . . . The yardstick of Christian love is the measure which should be used to evaluate the partial truths of pre-Christians.[3]

That the Hebrew Bible should be "taken on its face value" is precisely what we Jews insist. We reject and renounce the notion that it needs judgment by the yardstick of any other faith. We Jews resent this designation of our Bible. We call it the Hebrew Bible, not the Old Testament. The Christian Bible, then, consists of the Hebrew Bible plus the New Testament. Our annoyance is more than a case of quibbling. It reflects a refusal to accept second-class status for a living, functioning spiritual heritage. The snide undertones of the term "Old Testament" prepare the way for Arnold Toynbee's slanderous denigration of Judaism as a "fossil" religion.

There is a hint of condescension, if not of arrogance, in such statements. It is reflected as well in the way historic time is divided into *B.C.* and *A.D.—before Christ* and *in the year of our Lord.* The vast majority of earth's human population—at least two and a quarter billion of three billion—is not Christian; why should the calendar be calculated as if it were? Many—Jews and Christians alike—now refer to the customary epochs as *B.C.E.* and *C.E.—before the Common Era* and the *Common Era.*

The same motivation responsible for the designation "Old Testament" explains Christianity's libeling of the Pharisees. They are represented in the New Testament and subsequent church literature as hypocrites pompously concerned only with the letter of the law, not with its spirit. The fact of the matter is that the Pharisees were the democratically inclined majority of the Jewish people at the time of Jesus. They devoted themselves to extension and modification of basic, biblical Judaism through the development of talmudic literature. Their purpose was to keep Judaism flexible and vital, that it might continually adjust to new circumstances and new needs. The Pharisees were not perfect; no human beings are. But neither were they the depraved, pretentious hypocrites which Christian doctrine has made them out to be.

A glaring example of how specific Jewish teachings were distorted in order to enhance Christianity by contrast is the statement attributed to Jesus in the fifth chapter of Matthew: "Ye have heard that it was said, 'Thou shalt

love thy neighbor and hate thy enemy,' but I say unto
you, love your enemies." At no time, in no place, in no
manner, has Judaism ever said or implied that the enemy
was to be hated! Quite to the contrary, Jews are told in
Exodus that the enemy is to be aided if his animal is either
lost or overburdened. The book of Proverbs specifically
admonishes: "If thine enemy be hungry, give him bread
to eat; and if he be thirsty, give him water to drink." (See
Exodus 23:4f; Proverbs 20:22, 24:17, 29, 25:21f.) One
rabbi went so far as to say that even when an enemy
came to one's house to slay him, if he was hungry and
thirsty, he should be given food and drink!

Despite the cruelty of Pharaoh in subjecting the ancient
Israelites to slavery, despite his duplicity in time and again
breaking his promise to set them free, as we Jews celebrate
Passover each year we flick off a drop of wine from our
glasses at the mention of each plague inflicted on the
Egyptians, to indicate our sorrow that even an enemy had
to suffer in order for our ancestors to achieve freedom.
The Bible reports that when the Israelites finally reached
the safe side of the sea they began to sing a song of rejoicing. The Midrash adds that the angels too joined in song;
God immediately stopped them, saying, "Creatures of mine
are drowning in the sea, and you sing?" What impudence
to transpose so compassionate a teaching as this into the
alleged doctrine that enemies are to be hated!

Not only were some of Judaism's teachings misrepre-
sented, but others were plagiarized. When Jesus was asked
to summarize the greatest of the commandments, he deliberately quoted two injunctions from the Hebrew Bible:
"You must love the Lord your God with all your heart,
and with all your soul, and with all your might," and "You
must love your neighbor as yourself." (See Matthew 22:
37-40; Mark 12:29-31; Luke 10:27.) Jesus knew he was
citing Judaism. (See Leviticus 19:18 and Deuteronomy 6:5.)

Many of his followers have forgotten. Even in the most respectable of places these doctrines are described by people who are beyond suspicion of conscious prejudice as if they had originated with Jesus. When reference is made to "the Christian injunction, 'love thy neighbor as thyself,'" it seems to Jews that built into the very fabric of Christian thinking across the centuries has been a reluctance to credit the older brother for anything the younger brother learned from him.

Closely allied with the designation of the Hebrew Bible as the Old Testament is the frequent Christian assumption that Judaism stopped growing at or about the time of Jesus. It is sometimes stated explicitly, sometimes just quietly assumed, that the only legitimate historic or theologic function of Judaism was to prepare the way for the Christian faith. In its extreme form, this doctrine claims that Christianity is the only valid post-biblical fruition of Judaism. The latter is assumed to have stagnated since the close of its biblical period, with all further dynamic development having appeared only under Christian auspices.

No one who knows Judaism accurately would deny for a moment that its firmest foundations are in the Bible. But to equate the Judaism of the twentieth century with that of the first makes no better sense than to say that the Empire State Building consists only of its foundation and ground floor. Simultaneous with the development of Christian thought through the literature of the New Testament, there was further extension of Judaism through the successive development of the Mishnah, the Talmud, the Midrash, the Commentaries and Codes, and the major writings of rabbis and scholars to this very day. Judaism is the source, the continuing mainstream. Christianity and Islam are branches which have diverged from the mainstream. In some respects the river and its branches are similar; in others, they differ considerably. But the source did not cease after its initial purpose had been served. To understand Judaism, one must not only study the Bible, but carefully examine subsequent developments in post-biblical tradition. Today's living Judaism is the sum total of every authentically Jewish insight from the time of Abraham up to and including yesterday.

Christians are becoming increasingly aware of this. Although the old attitude branding Judaism as a petrified fossil is still all too prevalent, many church authorities have made progress on two fronts: they recognize that Judaism continued its development beyond the time of Jesus; and they perceive that Christianity can be accurately understood only in relationship to the Judaism from which it emerged.

Each of us is free to study Judaism and its several derivatives conscientiously and then to arrive at his own preference. It is absurd, however, for anyone to compare an artificially truncated Judaism to a consummated Christianity or Islam and to judge as if these were the only alternatives.

Historic distortions of the attitude of Judaism to Jesus go all the way back to his life and death. According to the Christian record, the villains responsible for betraying and crucifying Jesus were "the Jews." It seems to matter not at all that his earliest, most devoted followers were Jews, that the Jewish people of Palestine had by then lost all effective suzerainty to the Romans, that crucifixion was a Roman, not a Jewish, method of capital punishment, that Jews had no conceivable motive for killing one who claimed to be the messiah whom they had been awaiting with impatient passion, that no other pretended messiah before or since was murdered by them, or that, in the eyes of imperial Rome, Jesus was a potential revolutionary, a political rebel who was a clear and present danger to the empire.

A scholarly study by a non-Jewish historian (S. G. F. Brandon: *Jesus and the Zealots: A Study of the Political Factor in Primitive Christianity*, Scribner, 1968) argues persuasively that Jesus was a political activist, a militant leader in the rebellion against Rome. Such a role, incidentally, would be entirely consistent with the Jewish concept of the messiah. It would also supply a plausible motive for the crucifixion. The Jews of that time had reason to accept or reject Jesus, to believe or doubt his messiahship; they had no cause to wish or do him harm. If, as Dr. Brandon asserts, Jesus was in fact a militant rebel, Rome had good reason indeed to fear him and to get rid of him.

Why, then, is Jesus portrayed in the New Testament as a saintly, ethereal person much more interested in an imminent "kingdom of God" than in obliterating the iniquities of earthly kingdoms? Brandon's explanation is that here too the historic record was deliberately modified. He holds that the transformation of Jesus into an other-worldly visionary "was deliberate, purposed, and indeed, no less than the result of a conscious distortion of the historical facts by the authors of the Gospels, especially Mark." Writing in Rome, addressing himself to possible converts, anxious to cast Judaism and the Jews in a bad light, Mark exonerated the Romans and assigned major blame for the crucifixion to the Jews.

All this is ignored in blaming the crucifixion on "the Jews." Not even the pronouncements of Vatican II have corrected the record on this score. All that was acknowledged was that exclusive blame should not be assessed against all Jews living then or against the Jewish people living now. The inference remains that "the Jews" were responsible for a death which Christian theology has held to be predestined in any event.

Some Protestant spokesmen have been more forthright

than Vatican II in attempting to correct this aspect of the record. In December of 1961 the World Council of Churches referred to blame for the crucifixion as "responsibilities which belong to our corporate humanity and not to one race or community." At its Sixty-first General Convention the Protestant Episcopal Church stated:

> The charge of deicide against the Jews is a tragic mis-understanding of the inner significance of the crucifix-ion. . . . All men are guilty of the death of Christ, for all have in some manner denied Him; and since the sins that crucified Christ were common human sins, the Christian knows that he himself is guilty.

Such declarations as these represent honest efforts by the Christians who issue them to set this part of the record straight.

This important matter is of more than academic or his-toric interest. Competent scholars are agreed that Christian teaching about the crucifixion is one of the seminal causes of anti-Semitism. The first impression the average Chris-tian child receives of Jews—indeed, in many cases his first hearing of the very word *Jew*—is in connection with the life and death of Jesus. At once he associates the term with villainous scoundrels, allegedly responsible for inflicting cruelty and pain on "the Son of God." In later life all kinds of intellectual justifications and rationalizations are employed to account for a prejudice which was initially emotional and which originated with the story of the crucifixion.

The late John Haynes Holmes, an outstanding liberal Protestant, said that "the roots of anti-Semitism can easily be traced to the central dogma of the church. . . . This doctrine sets forth that the Jews rejected and crucified the Messiah, that thereby they were rejected of God and condemned to wander the earth as an outcast people. . . . This doctrine . . . for all practical purposes is still central in eighty-five to ninety per cent of the present-day church membership. . . . As long as this dogma dominates the theology of the churches and thereby influences the psychology and life of its millions of members, anti-Semitism cannot but be encouraged."[4] One may hope that the proportion of church membership which still subscribes to these notions has decreased since Dr. Holmes made his estimate, but a recent scholarly study, *Christian Beliefs and Anti-Semitism*, leads us to suspect that the essential truth of his assertion remains.[5]

It would be deplorable enough if the story of Jesus' death as recounted in the New Testament were historically accurate. What compounds the injustice immeasurably is that the gospel narrative cannot possibly be faithful to historical fact. The slightest knowledge of the Jewish practice and law of two millennia ago will prove this. According to the New Testament, Jesus was tried at night; Jewish law prohibited the Sanhedrin from meeting earlier than 6 A.M. The New Testament claims that Jesus was tried on the first night of Passover; no Jewish trial was permitted on the Sabbath or a festival. The gospels locate the trial at the high priest's home; in Jewish law all cases involving capital punishment were tried in a special chamber of the temple constructed for that very purpose. The New Testament describes the entire trial as occupying but a few hours, with the crucifixion following immediately. Rabbinic law clearly stipulated that any capital case must last at least two days, with one day each for the prosecution and the defense, and that the death sentence could not be executed on the same day it was pronounced. The judges of the Sanhedrin had to allow themselves a night's sleep and reflection on the sentence and reconsider it the next day. Any account which misrepresents strict legal practice in so many ways is, to say the least, distorted and inaccurate.

Because of their alleged complicity in this crime, at least
equally because they rejected the claim of messiahship on
Jesus' part, Jews have been branded through the centuries
as an accursed people, ordained by God to wander the
earth until they finally accept Christ fully. In their zeal
to establish the fact that the man of Nazareth was indeed
the messiah anticipated by Hebrew scripture, church
authorities have not refrained from deliberate mistransla-
tion. In the seventh chapter, fourteenth verse of Isaiah,
the prophet is made to declare: "And a virgin shall conceive." This is not what the words originally read or meant.
The Hebrew word used by Isaiah means *a young woman*,
virginal or not. If the prophet had meant *virgin*, he would
have used the proper Hebrew word for it. Recent English
translations of the New Testament have sought to correct
this centuries-old error.

Despite the best effort of Jesus' biographers to depict
him as the messiah Jews had foretold, there are discrepancies enough in their accounts to arouse considerable
doubt. This is important, because if Jesus was not in fact
the one awaited by Isaiah and his co-religionists, then it
was sheer nonsense to pretend that God would blame or
curse those who did not accept him. There is a growing
recognition of this truth today among Christian scholars.

These scholars are also making valiant efforts to redress
the wrongs of the past. For many centuries both Catholics
and Protestants have expended prodigious energy toward
converting Jews to Christianity, convinced that they were
thereby saving them from damnation and error, leading
them to salvation and redemption. In medieval times Jews
were forced to attend Christian church services and to
hear sermons urging them to accept Christianity. During
such historic periods as the Inquisition in fifteenth-century
Spain, the conversionary enterprise went beyond preach-
ing and persuasion to torture and force.

It would be irresponsibly naive to pretend that all attempts to convert Jews have ceased. Several national Christian organizations are still active along this line both on college campuses and in the larger community. But responsible Christian leaders are beginning to recognize that such endeavors are both fruitless and unfair. One of the more productive consequences of Vatican II was the formation of the International Catholic-Jewish Liaison Committee which held its sixth annual meeting in Venice on March 28, 1977.

A fascinating and extremely significant paper was read there by Professor Tomasso Federici, a faculty member at the Pontifical University of Propaganda Fide in Rome and an official consultant to the Vatican's Commission for Religious Relations with the Jews. Among the memorable statements he made were the following:

—The Church thus rejects in a clear way every form of proselytism . . .
> (Section II.A.13)

—Also excluded is every sort of judgment expressive of discrimination, contempt or restriction against the Jewish people as such, and against individual Jews as such or against their faith, their worship, their general and in particular their religious culture, their past and present history, their existence and its meaning . . .
> (Section II.A.14)

—. . . attempts to set up organizations of any sort, particularly educational or welfare organizations for the "conversion" of Jews must be rejected . . .
> (Section II.A.18)

We must neither ignore nor exaggerate the importance of such statements as these. At least for the time being, they represent the views of one Catholic theologian, not of the church officially. Such views, moreover, from both Catholic and Protestant scholars, have been expressed by only a small number of authorities. The masses of church-going Christians have not yet been touched by them, nor are they likely to be in the immediate future. If this new attitude were to permeate to all levels of Christian life, it could lead to a new and healthier relationship between Judaism and Christianity.

Christian tradition has also perpetrated the fiction that Judaism stresses a God of strict justice and vengeance, in contrast to its own benevolent deity of forgiveness and love. Rather than argue the point at length, however, suppose we list without identification a number of passages from the combined Hebrew and Christian Bible, descriptive of God or His traits:

1. "I the Lord your God am an impassioned God, visiting the iniquity of the fathers upon the children, upon the third and upon the fourth generations of those who reject Me . . ."
2. God orders the enemy to be slain, "both man and woman, infant and suckling."
3. "Fear Him who is able to destroy both body and soul in Gehenna."
4. "Whoever speaks against the Holy Spirit, there is no forgiveness for him whether in this world or the next."
5. "God is love; and he that abideth in love abideth in God."
6. It is God's will that "not one of these little ones shall perish."
7. God is "slow to anger and plenteous in mercy."
8. God shows "kindness to the thousandth generation of those who love Me and keep My commandments."
9. "The Lord is good to all, and near to all who call upon him."

Now it is easy enough to recognize that the first four of these quotations depict a harsh, vengeful God, while the last five give the impression of a God who forgives and loves. The temptation of many, if not most, Americans would probably be to guess that the first four were taken from the Hebrew Bible, the final five from the New Testament. Such guesses would be wrong. In fact, Hebrew scripture is the source for numbers 1, 2, 7, 8 and 9; the others are from the New Testament. Neither document has a monopoly on a concept of either a harsh or a kindly God. Both represent a variety of views. The variety is greater in the older Bible because its writing spanned some ten to fifteen centuries, compared to the much shorter period of 150 years for the books held especially sacred by Christians. To contrast only the unacceptable in one to a careful selection of the noble in the other is unreasonable and unfair. Yet this is precisely what much of the Western world has done at the expense of Judaism.

Closely allied to this inaccurate portrayal of God as only a vengeful deity in Jewish thought is the popular notion that Judaism emphasizes harsh justice at the expense of mercy and love. It is true that justice is a pre-eminent ideal in Judaism. The prophet spoke for the authentic tradition when he urged: "Justice, justice must you pursue!" But this was not a harsh, rigid, unfeeling kind of justice.

A rabbinic expositor understood this distinction when he observed that the creation of the universe "may be compared to a king who had some empty glasses. The king said: 'If I pour hot water into them they will crack; if I pour ice-cold water into them they will also crack.' What did the king do? He mixed the hot and the cold water together and poured it into them and they did not crack. Even so did the Holy One, praised be He, say, 'If I create the world on the basis of the attribute of mercy alone, the world's sins will greatly multiply. If I create it on the basis of the attribute of justice alone, how could the world endure? I will therefore create it with the attributes of both mercy and justice, and may it endure!' "

Not only were mercy and justice conjoined in the hierarchy of Jewish values, but where it became necessary to achieve a reasonable balance between them, a preference was clearly expressed for mercy. Thus God is quaintly described in Jewish tradition as praying, "May it be My will that My mercy will supersede My justice!"

Unseasoned mercy and love soon degenerate into sentimentality. Brittle, unmitigated justice is too coarse a nutrient for the human spirit. Judaism strives for a wholesome balance of the two: for justice tempered by love, for love reinforced by justice.

Is it true that, until the coming of Jesus, Judaism was devoid of love? The historical record sharply refutes this. Eight centuries before the time of Jesus the prophet Hosea spoke with impressive eloquence of God's love. He even employed the tragic details of his own marriage as a paradigm. Hosea's wife had been unfaithful to him; yet he found his love for her so great that he was unable to cast her aside. He preached that God's love for Israel will do no less; though they had been faithless to God time and again, He could not help but forgive and love them. It was this Hebrew prophet, writing in the Hebrew language, who proclaimed in the name of God:

> And I will betroth thee unto Me forever;
> Yea, I will betroth thee unto Me in righteousness,
>   and in justice,
> And in lovingkindness, and in compassion.
> And I will betroth thee unto Me in faithfulness;
> And thou shalt know the Lord. . . .
> How shall I give thee up, Ephraim?
> How shall I surrender thee, Israel? . . .
> My heart is turned within Me,
> My compassions are kindled together.
> I will not execute the fierceness of Mine anger,
> I will not return to destroy Ephraim;
> For I am God, and not man,
> The Holy One in the midst of thee,

And I will not come in fury . . .
I will heal their backsliding,
I will love them freely;
For mine anger is turned away from him.
I will be as the dew unto Israel;
He shall blossom as the lily,
And cast forth his roots as Lebanon.

Justice of necessity involves law. Coupled, therefore, with the charge that Judaism has emphasized justice excessively has often been the accusation that it puts undue stress on legality. Ostensibly the Apostle Paul rejected legalism, substituting inner spirit for external force. In due course, however, Christianity found it necessary to construct its own legal structure; its teachers and leaders had learned an indisputable lesson in human behavior.

If human beings were perfect, or even nearly perfect, they could perhaps dispense with law. So long as we remain far short of perfection, our inner desire to behave decently will require encouragement and discipline through external restraint, which is to say: law. A generation ago we momentarily supposed that children reared permissively, without discipline, would become happy, healthy adults. Psychologists and psychiatrists are now substantially agreed that this expectation was unwarranted. Children need discipline, provided it be reasonable, consistent, fair, and appropriate to the conduct being guided. In this respect, something of the child remains in every adult. Therefore, without law the ends of neither justice nor love can be secured.

It is true that law for its own sake can become so restrictive as to defeat the very purposes it was meant to serve: the encouragement of creativity and healthy growth. To suppose that those ends can be attained without law, however, is to be blind to reality. In this respect, today we confront the same dilemma as did Paul and his contemporaries in the first century C.E. We are warned again and again that it is impossible to legislate morality. The response of perceptive people has been that the opposite is at least equally true: it is impossible to achieve or sustain morality without law. Though legislation cannot directly affect how a person feels inwardly, it can control his behavior. In a curious but demonstrably effective way, our conduct influences our feelings, perhaps as much as it is motivated by them.

Judaism has understood this since its infancy. It has therefore insisted upon a system of law—not for its own sake, not as a substitute for the spirit, but as the indispensable means toward guiding us in our slow, faltering struggle to become more godlike.

It is important that the record be set straight. Judaism must not be judged either by the misstatements of its maligners or by those zealous protagonists whose devotion to their own faith has induced them to create a whipping boy for invidious comparisons. Like all great traditions, Judaism is entitled to realistic and accurate evaluation on the basis of what it has been and purposes to be.

This should not be an argument between Christians and Jews. Objective Christian scholars have been among the authorities disclaiming distortions of every point raised in this chapter and insisting on truth. Whatever the psychological motivations of those who founded the faith, Christianity today has no need to denigrate or disparage Judaism. It has developed a rich heritage, a major contribution to the welfare and culture of humanity. It can and should stand on its own considerable merits. Neither Christianity nor Judaism possesses the whole truth. They can supplement each other in the arena of thought and faith.

PART THREE
WHAT THE JEW DOES

CHAPTER SIX

First Things First

THUS FAR we have become acquainted with those insights concerning the nature of reality which came to the Jew by intuition and personal observation, and which he took for granted. It must be emphasized again that these assumptions were in a sense secondary. In Judaism action always counted more than speculation or theory. Nineteen centuries ago Rabbi Jochanan ben Zakkai expressed the priorities of his heritage with rare audacity: "If you are engaged in planting, and suddenly have been informed that the Messiah has arrived, finish with your planting first and then go greet him."[1]

Other authentic spokesmen for Judaism may have been less incisive but were equally clear. They emphasized time and again that our responsibility toward our fellows supersedes even that to God. Thus the Talmud, in commenting on the biblical story of the three strangers to whom Abraham offered such exemplary hospitality, noted that the patriarch had been conversing with God but broke off the moment he saw the strangers, in order that he might care for their needs.[2]

We shall shortly have something to say about the importance of study in Judaism, especially study of Torah. But study only for its own sake was rejected. Witness the following talmudic testimony:

He who occupies himself with the study of the Torah only is as if he had no God.

If a man studies the Torah without the intention of fulfilling it, it were better he had never been born.

Not the expounding of the Torah is the chief thing, but the doing of it.

There is little moral philosophy in Judaism, much moral admonition and injunction. Ethics are a very practical matter, a blueprint for structuring one's daily life, not a field for speculative theory. One chasid asked another what he had learned from his rabbi. Instead of answering in terms of sophisticated doctrine, the second replied, "How he laces his shoes."

Søren Kierkegaard, whose thought is basic to the movement known as religious existentialism, spoke of the "teleological suspension of the ethical." By that he meant that adherence to God's will need have nothing to do with ethical action, that sometimes in order to serve God best, we must do that which appears in our human judgment to be unethical. A brilliant twentieth-century rabbi, the late Milton Steinberg, gave the definitive answer of Judaism to such a proposal: "From the Jewish point of view . . . the ethical is never suspended, not under any circumstances and not for anyone, not even for God. Especially not for God!"[3]

For Kierkegaard, the story of Abraham's willingness to sacrifice Isaac (see Genesis 22:1-14) illustrates the fact that one must stand ready to do unethical things to prove his loyalty to God. To the Jew, this narrative symbolizes exactly the opposite conclusion. We interpret it to mean that Abraham was mistaken in believing that service to God necessitated the sacrifice of his son. For us, the important point of the episode is Abraham's realization at the end that God did not want such conduct—indeed, that there can be no conflict between ethics and God's will.

In some faiths it would be considered impudence for man

to challenge God on ethical grounds. In Judaism such behavior is standard procedure. Thus, when God was about to
destroy the cities of Sodom and Gomorrah because of their
inhabitants' wickedness (see Genesis 18:16-33) Abraham
demanded that He first ascertain whether there were not
righteous men there too. In a sentence which is characteristic of the uninterrupted stress which Judaism places on
ethical deeds, Abraham asks, "Shall not the Judge of all the
earth deal justly?"

Clearly, then, for Judaism the ethical deed is immeasurably more important than the theological tenet. Faith is
worth only as much as the way of life it stimulates. This is
what prompted a nineteenth-century rabbi to suggest the
possibility that a person who lives as God would want him to
"shall have done God's will even though he may, God forbid, deny the existence of God."[4]

As we have already noted, moreover, no area of life is
exempt from the divinely inspired ethical dictate. Within
the context of the Bible's agricultural economy, an ancient
rabbi pointed to this truth. He said there is a Jewish way of
doing everything. In plowing, we are warned that the ox and
ass must not be teamed together; in sowing, that certain
seeds should not be planted side by side; in reaping, that a
portion of the crop must be left for the poor; in threshing,
that the ox must not be muzzled while performing its task.[5]

In short, here in our section on ethics we come to the heart
of Judaism. For an understanding of the major directives of
Jewish ethics, however, a few additional preliminaries are
in order.

First, it should be noted that the preoccupation of Judaism with ethics is not a recent development; it existed even
in ancient times. Many shallow comparisons have been
made between the moral code propounded by Moses and the
ancient Babylonian Code of Hammurabi; some writers
have even suggested that Moses only copied the earlier

document. Careful study will disclose how untrue this is. The Hammurabi Code provides for inferior and superior social strata, with different degrees of responsibility attached to each. The punishment for knocking out the tooth of a common man is very much less than that for destroying the tooth of a nobleman. If a common man killed the pregnant daughter of his social equal, his own daughter was executed. A nobleman who caused the same death paid only an inconsequential fine. The ethics sponsored by Moses make no such distinctions between rich and poor, governors and governed, citizens and foreigners. All are treated and judged alike.

The Code of Hammurabi provides no punishment for injuring or even murdering a slave. Ancient Jewish standards judged such maltreatment severely. The Babylonians ordered death for one who helped a slave to escape or gave him refuge in his house. Moses decreed: "You shall not turn over to his master a slave who seeks refuge with you from his master. He shall live with you in any place he may choose among the settlements in your midst, wherever he pleases; you must not ill-treat him." Ancient Judaism enjoined upon its adherents an elaborate body of mandates providing special consideration and compassion for the stranger, the widow, the orphan, and the poor. No such concern was included by either Babylonians or Egyptians in their law codes.

Even some provisions which are occasionally used to brand the ethics of the Hebrew Bible as inferior actually attest to the opposite if they be properly understood. Ancient Judaism has been castigated, for example, because it upheld the standard of "life for life, eye for eye, tooth for tooth, hand for hand, foot for foot, burn for burn, wound for wound, bruise for bruise." What is frequently forgotten is that for the time in which these equations were initiated, they presented considerable ethical improvement. Among other peoples then, it was common to take in revenge a dozen lives or eyes or teeth for one. What Moses was really saying was that punishment must be commensurate with the offense, not unrestrictedly severe. Even before the close of the biblical period, moreover, this passage was interpreted to provide for financial rather than literal compensation, the basis for all modern law of damages.

There are still societies today which fall short of the ethical sensitivity of "eye for eye." As recently as July of 1977, for example, General Mohammad Zia ul-Haq, military ruler of Pakistan, issued a set of orders based on strict Islamic law. These decrees provided that a looter or thief may have his hands amputated or be sentenced to five years at hard labor. If armed, he is subject to amputation or death. A man who insults a woman, even by word, gesture or sound, may be punished by ten years of "rigorous imprisonment and/or whipping up to thirty stripes." Laws similar to these have been recently reinstituted and are being rigorously enforced also in Saudi Arabia. Such extremes of punitive harshness as these—and even worse— were commonplace in the ancient world. What may at first appear to be repressive in the laws of Moses was actually, if we examine it carefully and objectively, a step toward liberalizing the penal procedures of the time, making them more humane.

One additional general comment should precede a listing of specific ethical directives. In recent years we have heard much about so-called situation ethics. The core of this idea is that no rigid, hard-and-fast standards of right and wrong can be accepted in advance as absolute, to be applied without discrimination to all problems. That which is clearly right in one situation may be ambiguous or even entirely wrong in another.

Judaism has long understood the importance of tailoring ethical ideals to suit the case in hand. This flexibility becomes especially necessary when two or more valid ideals clash, so that it becomes impossible to strive for both. No one placed higher priority on truth than did the rabbis; yet they said that the truth should not be told to a dying patient whose pain would thereby be increased. They also decreed that truth can be withheld if the telling of it would cause friction between persons who would otherwise live together peacefully. They even boldly cited an instance from the Bible in which God Himself altered the truth in order not to create antagonism between Abraham and Sarah.

There is a crucial difference, however, between expediency and compromise. Judaism does not defend the sacrifice of an ideal for the sake of one's immediate personal advantage. It does recognize that in real life each ideal must be considered in a pantheon containing all valid ideals, and that a given situation will determine which standards are the most important at that moment. On one occasion it may be truth which should temporarily give way to mercy; the next time the priority may be reversed.

The situation ethicist is correct in asserting that no tradition can give us final, prearranged answers to every ethical dilemma. He is wrong if he implies that there are no valid standards. Judaism propounds a noble system of ethical values, in the composite light of which every individual problem must be evaluated. As we have noted, the broader directions of that system are indicated by the evolutionary process itself. Lest we immediately go astray, it should be emphasized that each of these directions is valid only in consideration of all the others. Any one of them pursued exclusively can cause more harm than good. *All else being equal*, the ethical action in any situation is that which will increase organization and order, enhance cooperation rather than competition, promote individuality instead of conformity, enlarge freedom and expand spiritual progress for the individuals concerned.

The modern Jew is not inclined to believe that a given course of action is true because Moses recommended it. He prefers to put the sequence oppositely: Moses recommended it because it was true. A genius in the physical sciences is one who discovers a characteristic of the material universe which was previously unknown. A spiritual genius is one who is first to discover an aspect of cosmic moral law. Moses was such a genius, as were many others in the subsequent development of Judaism. Their combined accomplishment cannot give us sure or certain answers to every dilemma we face; but it can provide reliable guidelines, which we must interpret and apply in each instance ourselves.

Perhaps the most central of these guidelines is the idea of holiness. In any other religious tradition, such a concept as holiness would have been discussed in the section on beliefs. It is characteristic of Judaism that instead we consider it here, as part of "What the Jew Does."

Nowhere is this notion more eloquently phrased than in the nineteenth chapter of Leviticus, which orders: "You shall be holy, for I, the Lord your God, am holy!" What does it mean in Judaism for a man or woman to achieve holiness? Not to assume artificial mannerisms or wear exceptional clothing or withdraw from ordinary pursuits. Leviticus leaves no mystery; it immediately outlines what a person must do if he is successfully to emulate God's holiness. He must revere his parents, leave the gleanings of his harvest for the poor, desist from stealing or lying, pay his workers promptly, give special consideration to the handicapped, execute justice equally for rich and poor, avoid vengeance—and above all—love his neighbor as himself. This is what holiness must mean for the Jew.

A rabbi quoted in the Talmud makes this clear. Asked what "You shall be holy" means, he replied, "It means that when you are weighing a pound of meat, it should weigh a pound." The quest for holiness cannot be a part-time or casual occupation. In urging it upon his followers, a chasidic rabbi advised them to emulate thieves, who toil far into the night and at great risk to accomplish their work.

All this makes it evident that the Jew who would know how to attain holiness must know not only the Bible, but also talmudic and chasidic literature and much more. No other human tradition has valued study and knowledge for the masses of its people as highly as Judaism. Indeed, learning was an imperative! We are told that "an ignorant man cannot be a pious man"; that "he who learns from his fellowman even a single chapter, a single rule, a single verse, a single expression, or a single letter, ought to pay honor to such an individual"; that "he who does not increase his knowledge decreases it." We are urged: "Let your house be a meeting place for the wise. Sit among them when they study and listen carefully to their wisdom." In answer to the query "Who is wise?" we are told: "He who learns from everyone."[6]

In Jewish life study has always been considered a form of worship. Between the daily afternoon and evening services in the synagogue, the worshipers occupied themselves with study. On Sabbath afternoon, having spent the whole morning in prayer, they returned to hear a visiting preacher expound on the meaning of a significant Torah portion. According to Jewish law a synagogue could be sold if necessary in order to acquire a school; the transaction in reverse was not allowed.

Such preoccupation with knowledge must not be taken for granted. The prominent Moslem authority Abu Sa'id once exclaimed, "Books! Ye are excellent guides, but it is absurd to trouble about a guide after the goal has been reached." The first step in Sufism, mystical sect of Islam, calls for "the breaking of ink-pots and the tearing up of books and the forgetting of knowledge." Echoes of such petulance are to be found in the anti-intellectualism of certain modern religious postures too. To the Jew who knows Judaism, they are scandalous.

Contrast the foregoing words of Abu Sa'id to those of Maimonides: "Every Jew is obligated to study Torah whether he be poor or rich, in good physical health or a sufferer, young or very old. Even if he goes begging from door to door, and has a wife and children to support, he must set aside time for the study of the Torah. . . . And how long must he continue to study? Until his death."

Because of the high value their tradition assigns to study, modern Jews have established elaborate systems for the Jewish education of their children. Contemporary educators and rabbis are increasingly dissatisfied with the one-session-a-week religious school to which some parents send their children on Saturday or Sunday morning. Such classes do not provide enough time for instruction in the ingredients for intelligent participation in Jewish life: history, ethics, faith, the Hebrew language, literature, holidays, rituals, Jewish communal institutions and problems.

Most congregations achieve a more adequate level of education by requiring their students to attend classes three times a week—once on a weekend morning and on two weekday afternoons following their secular school session. Some congregations and community schools operate five sessions a week supplementary to the child's secular education. In recent years, dissatisfied with the results attained even by these systems, small but significant numbers of Jews have turned to the Jewish day school as a solution. Here students attend a school under private Jewish sponsorship all day, concentrating on the normal public school curriculum for half the day and on their Jewish studies the other half.

Adult education is probably the weakest link in the chain of American Jewish pedagogy. Despite occasional notable

successes, programs of adult Jewish studies are too super-
ficial and shallow. Intense competition for his time in a
hurried and harried civilization, plus the many demands
for continuing vocational or professional study, make it
ever more difficult for the average adult to remain Jewishly literate. Sensitive Jewish leaders must always be alert,
however, to the responsibility for a lifetime of learning
which their tradition imposes upon them.

The overarching purpose of study in Judaism was the
discovery of truth, for, according to the Talmud, truth is
the seal of God.[7] The commentators were quick to point
out that the Hebrew word for *truth*(אמת)is spelled with
the first(א), the last(ת), and the middle letters (מ) of the
alphabet. Truth is all-encompassing.

Because of its concentration on study and truth, the attitude of Judaism toward science has been unique among religious traditions. An episode like the recantation of Gal-
ileo forced by the Catholic Church, or the trial of Scopes
by fundamentalist Protestantism because he taught evolution, would be unthinkable within Judaism. Our tradition
does not impose upon us a blind, unthinking faith which
bears no relationship to facts disclosed by science. While
religion can and must accept as truth that which goes beyond the demonstrable evidence of science, it should not
subscribe to any doctrine which science clearly proves to
be impossible or absurd.*

In Jewish eyes the scientist is employing the skills at
which he is most adept to discover ever more perceptively
how God created and operates the universe. Both the Bible
and the Talmud contain many passages reflecting the most
accurate scientific observations available to the writers.

It is no coincidence that throughout the Middle Ages so
many eminent Jews participated in the sciences, especially
medicine. Maimonides, the twelfth-century savant to whom

* See pp. 37ff.

we have made frequent reference, was a physician of international repute. He wrote extensively on poisons and their antidotes, on sexual intercourse, asthma, and many aspects of hygiene. He wrote that God can be truly known only if there is free study of both physics and metaphysics, which means to say, of science as well as philosophy and religion.[8] Maimonides was once asked by a skeptic what Jews could do if science were ever to discover that the universe is eternal. This, after all, would conflict with the biblical teaching that at a particular moment of time God created the universe. The answer of Maimonides was: "In that event, we would have to try to understand the Torah better!"[9] Here was a rejection of neither religion nor science; rather an enlightened understanding of the fact that they must operate together.

In the twelfth century, even as now, there were some religionists who supposed that every word of scripture—even allusions to history and science—was literally true. To them Maimonides said, "We must not expect that everything our sages say respecting astronomical matters should agree with observation, for mathematics was not fully developed in those days. Their statements were not based on the authority of the prophets, but on the imperfect knowledge which they themselves possessed or derived from scientists of their time. . . . In scientific matters everyone should act according to the results of his own study and accept that which appears to him established by proof."

A generation later one of the most illustrious of rabbis also stood among the foremost scientists of his time. Gersonides (Levi ben Gerson) declared that a student of science must not be hampered by preconceived religious notions, adding, "The Torah is not a code that compels us to believe in falsehoods." He too was asked by a contemporary what should be done if an apparent contradiction is uncovered between the Torah and science. He replied

that both would require re-examination.[10] It might be that
we had not correctly understood the Torah or that our
scientific reasoning had been faulty; only the most scrupulous study could disclose which was the case.

It is due to this spirit of free and open inquiry, this
eagerness to welcome knowledge and truth from all sources,
that Judaism never suffered an agonizing conflict between
itself and the new discoveries of science. For the same reason, a greatly disproportionate number of Jews may be
found to this day among practicing and research physicians
and in the several teaching disciplines of science.

We have already caught incidental glimpses of the tremendous consideration and compassion with which Jews
have been adjured by tradition to treat their fellows. No
trace of self-abnegation, however, was ever condoned.
With impeccable psychological insight, anticipating much
of modern awareness, even the ancient authorities of Judaism realized that he who does not respect himself cannot
possibly respect or love others. Leviticus therefore commanded that the Jew must love his neighbor *as thyself*,
not *more than thyself*. In the first century before the Common Era, Hillel uttered one of the most frequently quoted
pronouncements in Judaism: "If I am not for myself, who
will be for me?"

The Talmud poses the hypothetical case of two men lost
in a desert. Only one of them carries a flask, in it enough
water to keep but one person alive. What is the ethical
thing for the owner of the canteen to do? Some rabbis
answered that he should share, even though it would mean
that both would perish. But the greatest authority of his
time, Rabbi Akiba, said that it would be better for one to
drink and be saved than for both to die because of misguided sentimentality. In general, Judaism sees nothing
ethically wrong in the owner's saving himself; his life is
worth no less than any other. The exception would be if,

for example, his companion happened to be a great teacher. Only then would it be incumbent upon him to sacrifice himself so that the person who had more to contribute to posterity might survive.[11]

Because Judaism enjoins its adherents to value their own lives, it preaches no doctrine of "turn the other cheek." This is in any event an impossible ethic. It asks of the average person more than he is constitutionally able to give—perhaps even more than he should be willing to give. For acquiescence in this kind of self-denial can lead to gross injustice.

Dr. Joseph Klausner, probably the greatest Jewish scholar on Jesus, wrote: ". . . what room is there in the world for justice if we must extend both cheeks to our assailants and give the thief both cloak and coat?" Supine surrender to aggression can even encourage expressions of sadism. Certain types of pathological individuals relish cruelty especially when the victim proves to be willingly helpless. Judaism insists that the enemy be treated fairly, that he be given water to slake his thirst and food to mitigate his hunger. It does not expect or ask that he be loved.

A careful reading of the New Testament will reveal that not even Jesus, who allegedly originated the admonition to turn the other cheek, actually practiced it. He called those of whom he disapproved "blind fools," "a brood of vipers," "hypocrites and serpents." On at least one occasion, while overturning the tables of the Temple's moneychangers, he resorted to violence.

Judaism cannot and will not approve injustice, whether it be directed at another or oneself. It teaches that injustice and evil must be resisted.

Only half of Hillel's statement was quoted a few paragraphs back. After asserting, "If I am not for myself, who will be for me?" he added, "and if I am only for myself, what am I?" Concern only for others is masochism; regard only for myself is narcissism. Judaism condones neither. It insists that precisely because I cherish and value myself, I must feel no less for others. Though I am permitted to save myself if only my life or another's can be preserved, I am not allowed to kill a third person in order to keep myself alive. The Talmud is explicit: if A threatens to kill B unless B kills C, B must refuse. In either event an innocent life will be lost; "Who is prepared to say that your blood is redder than that of your proposed victim?"[12]

Judaism severely castigates those who stand idly by while harm is done to an innocent person. It stipulates that he who had it in his hand to do good and failed is equated with him who actually accomplished harm. Rabbinic law decrees that if a man sees someone drowning or being attacked by wild beasts or accosted by robbers, he is obligated to save the victim.

In the words of the Talmud: "I am a creature of God and my neighbor is also His creature; my work is in the city and his is in the field; I rise early to my work and he rises early to his. As he cannot excel in my work, so I cannot excel in his work. But you may be tempted to say: 'I do great things and he small things.' We have learned that it matters not whether one does much or little, if only he directs his heart to serve the divine purpose."[13]

Such compassionate consideration for others extends even to the lowliest servant. The Jew is warned not to eat fine bread while giving black bread to his servant, not to sleep on soft cushions while forcing him to sleep on straw. Small wonder that our tradition concludes: "He who has acquired a servant has acquired a master."[14]

Even more remarkable is the fact that in Judaism such kindness and consideration are due even to animals. The tradition speaks of *tza-ar ba-alay chayeem*, "the pain of all that lives." Reference has already been made in passing to the fact that the Torah prohibits muzzling an ox while it is treading grain. The reason is that the animal may be hungry, and it should not be forced into proximity with food, yet prevented from eating. An ox and an ass are not to be yoked together for plowing. The reason is that the ox is stronger than the ass, and putting them together might subject the ass to undue strain. The young of any animal is not to be removed from its mother for any reason during the first week following birth. One is strictly forbidden from capturing both a mother bird and its offspring on the same day. The Talmud adds to these biblical injunctions that the owner of an animal is not to eat first, before feeding his beast.

The customary blessing recited the first time a Jew wears new clothing is not recited over shoes because it was necessary to kill an animal for the leather. Nor is it repeated over a fur coat, for the same reason. We are told of one chasidic rabbi who was unable even to shout at a horse, another who went about offering water to thirsty calves at the market, a third who was unable to pass a bird cage without opening it to free the occupant. To this day hunting is an extremely rare sport among Jews. A modern European rabbi, asked by the Jewish owner of an estate whether it was permissible for him to hunt on his own property, responded, "I am surprised that you were moved to ask such a question. We find in the Torah the sport of hunting imputed only to such fierce characters as Nimrod and Esau, never to any patriarchs or their descendants. . . . I cannot comprehend how a Jew could even dream of killing animals for the pleasure of hunting, when he has no immediate need for the bodies of the creatures. . . ."

For many centuries Jews have called themselves *rach-maneem b'nay rach-maneem*—merciful descendants of merciful ancestors. The compassionate teachings of their tradition justify this appellation.

Do all Jews abide fully by the ethical precepts of Judaism? Of course not. Jews are human beings; no human being is infallible or perfect. Woodrow Wilson once said that the value of having a goal is that we can always know by how far we have failed to achieve it. The ethical ideals of Judaism are a constant challenge to the Jew, a reminder of what he must strive to be and do. Even if he were some day to reach the ideal as he now conceives it, by then his ethical sensitivity would have become so enriched that a yet nobler vision would emerge on his horizon.

Despite our imperfections, however, we Jews believe there is such a thing as a characteristically Jewish way to behave. Elie Wiesel has described it poignantly in telling us how the Jewish prisoners in Buchenwald acted in April of 1945 when they were liberated. This, remember, was after months or years of cruel imprisonment and after six million of their fellow Jews had been brutally murdered.

> When the first American jeeps appeared at the gates, there were no outbursts of joy; the inmates did not have the strength left to rejoice. They looked and looked at their liberators; they looked out but they could not see; their eyes still held the image of the 60,000 prisoners taken away the preceding week. Then something happened: a few Russian POW's grabbed some jeeps and machine-guns and raced to Weimar, the neighboring town, and opened fire at will. They needed vengeance before they needed food. And what did the Jewish inmates do to prove they were free? Believe it or not, they held services . . . To tell Him: listen, as mere mortals, as members of the human society, we know we should seize weapons and use them in every place and in every way and never stop. Because it is our right. But we are Jews and as such we renounce that right; we choose—yes, choose to remain human. And generous.[15]

CHAPTER SEVEN

On Sex and Marriage

NOWHERE IS the distinctiveness of Jewish ethics more impressively implemented than in connection with sex and marriage. The repudiation of Original Sin, the insistence that body and soul are one, that the sacred is to be infused into the mundane, that every human experience must be pervaded with sanctity—all these converge in the Jewish approach to sex.

Augustine understood the Original Sin to have been sexual. He said that the transmission of guilt from Adam to succeeding generations occurred "through the sexual act, which by virtue of the lust that accompanies it, is inherently sinful." These words were an attempt to clarify an attitude which had long before become part of Christian tradition, a view which goes back to the Apostle Paul. Although Paul conceded that most men, lacking the self-control to remain celibate, needed marriage, and that husbands and wives should not deny each to the other sexually, he was also author of such statements as the following:

> To the unmarried and the widows I say that it is well for them to remain single as I do. But if they cannot exercise self-control, they should marry. For it is better to marry than to be aflame with passion.
> Yet those who marry will have worldly troubles, and I would spare you that.

So that he who marries his betrothed does well; and he who refrains from marriage will do better.[1]

Paul's rejection of sex has been explained by Christian apologists as a consequence of his conviction that God's kingdom was at hand and all mundane matters were to be placed in limbo awaiting this magic transformation. The mere fact, however, that the consummation of the divine plan was envisaged as minimizing the importance of sex or repudiating it totally tells us something of significance about Paul's view of sex.

Classic Christianity's preference for sexual abstinence is reflected in the decree of several sects that members of the clergy must remain virginal or celibate. This is consistent with the statement attributed to Jesus, in which he praised those who "make themselves eunuchs for the kingdom of heaven's sake."

The Pauline stance on sex carried over for centuries as the mainstream approach of Christianity. Even the use of cosmetics by women was discouraged. Tertullian, Roman Christian theologian of the late second and early third centuries, went so far as to insist that natural, unadorned feminine beauty "ought to be obliterated by concealment and neglect, since it is dangerous to those who look upon it." Within marriage, too, intercourse was discouraged unless undertaken for the express purpose of conceiving a child. Thus Jerome: "He who loves his wife too ardently is an adulterer." Augustine: "Intercourse even with one's legitimate wife is unlawful and wicked where the conception of offspring is prevented." Aquinas: "Every carnal act done in such a way that generation cannot follow is a vice against nature and a sin ranking next in gravity to homicide."

In a way, nature—or God—had betrayed the Church Fathers by associating procreation with the pleasures of sex. Nowhere is this more apparent than in Augustine's projection of his own wishful thinking into his doctrine that in

Paradise men would sow their seed in women with the same calm dispassion that marks a farmer's planting of seed in the furrows of his field![2]

As recently as 1952 Pope Pius XII castigated those "who, be they priests or laymen, preachers, speakers or writers, no longer have a single word of approbation or praise for the virginity devoted to Christ; who for years, despite the church's warnings and in contrast with her opinion, give marriage a preference in principle over virginity."[3] The foregoing is but a small part of the evidence which motivated one contemporary psychiatrist, Dr. Abraham N. Franzblau, to say, ". . . guilt forms a canopy over every Christian bed."

Recently there has been substantial change in the attitude of many Christian denominations and authorities regarding sex and marriage. Such change has understandably been speedier and more substantial among Protestants than among Catholics, though significant revision is occurring even in the Roman tradition.

One of the boldest contemporary Christian statements on sex is *Human Sexuality: New Directions in American Catholic Thought*, published in 1977 by The Catholic Theological Society of America. True, its suggestions and conclusions are far from being official church doctrine; indeed, they were summarily and speedily rejected by many. Yet they represent new winds blowing on some of the mists which have previously obscured the realities of sex in the bogs of Christian doctrine. The Catholic experts—religious and lay—who issued this volume acknowledge that "Christianity looks forward to a fulfillment in which sexuality and sexual pleasure are explicitly excluded (Mark 12:25)," and that "abstinence from sexual pleasure has been seen as an anticipation of that future fulfillment (1 Corinthians 7), and passionate desire for pleasure as contrary to holiness (1 Thessalonians 4:5)."[4]

The new insights on sex expressed with such refreshingly open honesty in this memorable volume are much closer to the historic values of Judaism than to those which have previously characterized Christianity. What are these Jewish values?

Well, to begin with, there is an open, unabashed acceptance of sex in Hebrew scripture. Both the approved and condemned sexual activities of the patriarchs are described freely. The attempt of Potiphar's wife to seduce Joseph, King David's adultery and the punishment incurred because of it, his son Amnon's rape of his half-sister Tamar—these are among the many honest references to sex in our Bible. Laws and norms governing menstruation are spelled out in both Bible and Talmud; an entire tractate is devoted to the subject in the latter. *Song of Songs*—later allegorized by both Judaism and Christianity—was undoubtedly in origin a series of erotic, passionate pagan love songs. The fact that such verses were included in sacred scripture discloses much about the ancient Jewish attitude toward sex. It was customary, moreover, for husbands to read *Song of Songs* to their wives on Sabbath evening.

The high priest was not permitted to perform his sacerdotal functions in the temple on the holiest day of the year, *Yom Kippur*, unless he was married. The record reveals only one eminent talmudic rabbi who was not married, and he felt constrained to apologize for his bachelorhood. The Talmud discusses in detail the best night of the week for husbands and wives to enjoy intercourse. It is not without significance that the night recommended, especially for scholars and their spouses, was the Sabbath.[5] One medieval rabbi justified this on the basis that a holy act should be performed on a holy day. It should be remembered that these volumes were not kept under lock and key or permitted only restricted circulation. They were freely available to all—indeed, were studied by young men as part of their education. The following passage is from the *Shulchan Aruch*, great sixteenth-century compendium of rabbinic law, by which Orthodox Judaism is governed to this day:

Each man is obliged to perform his marital duty according to his strength and according to his occupation. Gentlemen of leisure should perform their marital obligation every night. Laborers who are employed in the city where they reside should perform their duty twice weekly, but if they are employed in another city, once a week. Donkey-drivers [should have marital relations] once a week; camel-drivers, once in thirty days; sailors, once in six months. As for scholars, it is obligatory for them to have intercourse once a week, and it is customary for this to be Friday nights.

Lest it be inferred that only the needs of men were taken into consideration, it is elsewhere prescribed that a man should not depart for a long journey without having intercourse with his wife, and that the experience is to be repeated as soon as possible after his return. Refusal to cohabit was considered proper grounds for either a husband or a wife to sue for divorce.

Maimonides was apparently of two minds on the subject of sex. In one passage he expresses a view which seems much closer to the Christian than to the Jewish position, saying, "The act is too base to be performed except when needed." He places himself much more firmly within Jewish tradition elsewhere in writing: "The sexual union should be consummated only out of desire and as the result of the joy of the husband and wife. . . . He must not approach her when he thinks of another woman and certainly not when he is under the influence of alcohol or while they are quarreling, and hatred divides them. He must not approach her against her will or force her to submit to him out of fear." This final sentence echoes a view voiced in the Talmud many centuries earlier: "He who coerces his wife will produce unworthy children."

One of the most revealing passages on sex within the Jewish tradition has long been attributed to the thirteenth-century rabbinic scholar Nachmanides. Whoever or whatever its source, the statement expresses the authentic Jewish attitude accurately and sensitively:

> We who are the descendants of those who received the sacred Torah believe that God, blessed be He, created everything as His wisdom dictated, and He created nothing containing obscenity or ugliness. For if we were to say that intercourse is obscene, it would follow that the sexual organs are obscene. . . . And how could God, blessed be He, create something containing a blemish or obscenity, or a defect; for we would then find that His deeds are not perfect. . . . Before Him there is neither degradation nor obscenity; He created man and woman, fashioning all their organs and setting them in their proper function, with nothing obscene in them.[6]

There was neither reluctance nor reticence in the acceptance of marriage by Judaism. Celibacy was never extolled, neither for the clergy nor the laity. The unmarried person was considered to be incomplete. A man was not judged fully a man, nor a woman entirely a woman, unless married. One ancient rabbi proclaimed, "He who has no wife remains without good, without a helper, without joy, without a blessing." A colleague added, "He is not a whole man." Even more daring is the statement of yet another, "The unmarried man diminishes the likeness of God." In similar spirit a medieval Jewish mystic declared, "The Shechinah [God's Presence] can rest only upon a married man, because an unmarried man is but half a man, and the Shechinah does not rest upon that which is imperfect."

Jewish tradition associated love and marriage with God Himself. A rabbinic legend recounts that God creates each soul in two parts, one half to be placed in the body of a male, the other in that of a female. Marriage means that the two halves of a single soul—created together, meant for each other—are reunited in accordance with God's plan. In another rabbinic tale we are told that God thought His creation of the universe was completed after He had fashioned Adam. He was disturbed, however, by a note of discord which marred the harmony of the spheres. An angel whom He sent to investigate reported that the annoyance was caused by Adam's sigh of loneliness. Then God created Eve as Adam's partner; the discord disappeared—the work of creation was really finished. In the same vein an ancient rabbi, when asked by a Roman woman how God has occupied himself since completing Creation, responded that He spends His time matching couples for marriage.

We are told also that the wedding of Adam and Eve was celebrated with divinely catered circumstance and pomp. God Himself attired and adorned the bride, then pronounced the marriage blessings. The angels witnessed the ceremony, embellishing it with music and dance. Needless to say, most Jews today do not take these tales literally. They accept them as poetic expressions of the very high and enduring importance our tradition attaches to marriage.

We have already encountered the immense importance Jewish tradition assigns to study. How remarkable, then, is this passage from the Talmud: "A man shall first take unto himself a wife and then study Torah." The only purpose justifying the sale of a Torah scroll was to make marriage possible for an orphan who would otherwise have been too poor to marry.

A touching rabbinic parable addresses itself to the fact that marriage imposes certain restrictions on the freedom previously enjoyed by each partner while he was single. We are told that one day an emperor said to Rabbi Gamaliel, "Your God is a thief, because it is written [in Genesis]: 'The Lord God cast a deep sleep upon Adam and he slept; and He took one of his ribs.' " The rabbi's daughter had overheard the conversation. She asked her father to let her reply, and he agreed. The following day she entered a complaint with the emperor that thieves had broken into her home, taking a silver vessel and leaving a gold one. "Would that such a thief visited me every day!" exclaimed the emperor. The girl then replied, "Was it not, then, a splendid thing for the first man when a single rib was taken from him and a wife was supplied in its stead?" Such a statement indicates how eagerly Judaism accepted marriage as one of God's richest blessings, not as a concession to either unfortunate human passion or biological necessity.

We have already noted that—quite remarkable for the time—Judaism long centuries ago recognized the sexual needs of woman. What status did it assign to women generally? Some advocates of the women's movement have contended that in Jewish thought women were adjudged as inferior to men. This contention, in truth, is not altogether wrong; but neither is it fully correct. The fact is that historic Judaism demonstrates considerable ambivalence toward women. Even before inquiring into the specifics of this ambivalence, however, it should be noted that ancient Judaism was far superior in this respect to many other cultures. Aristotle, for example, one of the greatest of Greek thinkers, called women "deficient males." All that a Moslem need do to divorce his wife is to repeat three times before witnesses: "I hereby divorce you."

The early Christian church also denigrated the importance and role of women. Many of its theologians attributed the origin of sin to Eve. Tertullian, addressing women generally as Eve's descendants, tells them, "*You* are the Devil's gateway." Clement of Alexandria, who treats women far more fairly than others of the Church Fathers, nevertheless says they should blush for shame "when you think of what nature you are."[7] It is against such views as these that the attitudes of early Judaism must be judged.

The painful uncertainty of Judaism toward women can be traced all the way back to the story of creation in Genesis. There are two such stories, one related in Genesis 1:26–31, the other in 2:18–24. According to the first account, man and woman were created simultaneously and equally: "And God created man in His image, in the image of God He created him; male and female He created them." In the second story woman is brought into being almost as an afterthought and for the comfort and convenience of man. After observing that "it is not good for man to be alone," God decides to make "a fitting helper for him . . . So the Lord God cast a deep sleep upon the man and he slept; and He took one of his ribs and closed up the flesh at that spot. And the Lord God fashioned into a woman the rib that He had taken from the man, and He brought her to the man."

Just as the two creation accounts are inconsistent in their evaluation of women, so Jewish thought in subsequent centuries yields evidence on both sides of the question. The Talmud describes a woman who complained to Rabbi Judah that her husband had treated her abominably. The rabbi is reported to have responded: "Why are you different from a fish? You have no more right to complain against your husband's treatment than the fish has a right to object to the manner in which it has been cooked."

Rabbinic law prohibits a man from marrying a woman whom he has not seen lest he later find her repulsive. No such restriction was imposed upon a woman, however, for "no matter how ugly or repelling the husband may turn out to be, she will surely be satisfied since to be married to a man, be he ever so loathsome, is better than to remain a spinster."

Perhaps the most unacceptable of all denigrations is the blessing pronounced each morning by traditionally observant Jewish males: "Praised be the Eternal our God,

Ruling Spirit of the universe, who did not make me a woman." This blessing bothered many of our medieval commentators who proceeded to mitigate its harshness. They said that the man who thanked God for making him a male was no more downgrading women than the priest who voiced gratitude for having been made a priest meant to disparage others.

In both cases, we are told, the concept of *mitzvah*—of special religious responsibility—is involved. For the faithful Jew a *mitzvah*, while of course entailing extra obligation and burden, gives one the privilege of serving God in special ways. The priest expressed appreciation for the fact that he was permitted to perform *mitzvot* beyond those assigned to other Jews; this did not mean that he judged himself to be innately superior to them. Similarly, the rabbis insisted, men were grateful for the fact that they had to fulfill certain *mitzvot* of which women were absolved because of other important responsibilities. It would be unrealistic to deny that there must have been men who misinterpreted this formula to imply male superiority. Judaism at its best, however, was as uncomfortable with any such notion as we are today.

Evidence of our tradition's favorable attitude toward women includes the fact that two books of our Hebrew Bible are named after women, that the matriarchs and Moses' sister Miriam are assigned major roles in the biblical narrative, that the Talmud enumerates forty-eight male and seven female prophets in the early stages of Jewish history.

Regarding numerous incidents in the Torah, high praise is heaped by later commentators upon women. We are told that the faith of women during the Egyptian slavery exceeded that of men and that the Exodus from Egypt was granted as a reward for their righteousness. According to an ancient *midrash*, before God gave the Torah in detail to the men at Sinai, He enunciated its basic principles to the women. Another *midrash* asserts that, when Aaron was about to make the Molten Calf, the women of Israel refused to contribute their golden jewelry for this purpose. It was only after the men had given theirs that Aaron was able to proceed. Later the women reminded Moses of their virtue in this respect when he was at first reluctant to accept their gifts for the building of the wilderness sanctuary. Thus reminded, Moses acceded to their request and accepted their contributions.

When God decided in exasperation to destroy the Temple because of the people's repeated sins, tradition tells us that the patriarchs, Moses, and the prophets all interceded in vain. It was only after Rachel implored Him that He agreed eventually to bring His people back to the land they were about to lose.

In Judaism, woman's charity is judged to be more direct than man's, her prayers are answered first, and she exercises the dominant moral influence on the family. To illustrate the latter truth, our rabbis told the following tale:

> It is related of a pious man who was married to a pious woman that, being childless, they were divorced. He married a wicked woman and she made him wicked. She married a wicked man and made him righteous. It follows that all depends upon the woman.

Women clearly suffered an inferior status in Jewish law and ritual observance. Except for certain special cases, women were not accepted as witnesses in a trial and did not inherit equally with their male siblings. They were not expected to perform most of the daily religious duties or recite the many blessings assigned to men; they had to sit by themselves in a special section in the balcony of the synagogue.

The segregation of women in the synagogue is of relatively recent origin; even many Jews are unaware of that.

The earliest synagogues separated women from men during public worship only when they were crowded on the major holidays, even then only by a row of pottery or sticks. Formal and more pronounced separation of the sexes did not begin until the thirteenth century.

Absolving women from some of the religious duties incumbent upon men can be interpreted as either discrimination or privilege. Most authorities on Judaism adopted the latter view. They agreed that it would be grossly unfair to hold women responsible for a whole schedule of duties which had to be performed at specific times during the day, thus conflicting with the needs and demands of their children. One modern observer summarizes this approach admirably in saying, "Not even an angel is given two missions simultaneously."

If women were prohibited from performing the *mitzvot* assigned to men, that would be rank discrimination. The fact is, however, that they were *excused*, not *prohibited*. The distinction was clear to a medieval commentator:

> We do not prevent women from reciting the blessing over the *lulav* and the *sukkah*.* The fact that the Talmud says that women are free from positive commandments that are fixed by time means merely to specify that they are not in duty bound to obey those commandments, but, if a woman desires to fulfill these commandments, she may do so and we do not prevent her . . .

In modern Jewish life much is being done to remove the ambiguities of Jewish tradition vis-à-vis women. *Bat Mitzvah* is an example. Since the fourteenth century Jewish boys have been initiated into religious adulthood on the Sabbath following their thirteenth birthdays.** Today

* The lulav is the palm branch used during the festival of Sukkot (see p. 152f.); the sukkah is the booth in which observant Jews take their meals at that time.
** See p. 156.

most Conservative and Reform congregations conduct a similar ceremony for girls. *Bar Mitzvah* means son of commitment or responsibility; *Bat Mitzvah* means daughter of commitment or responsibility.

In Reform and many Conservative congregations today women are counted in the *minyan*, the quorum of ten needed for a public worship service, and are called to the pulpit for *aliyot** during the Torah service. A number of women—mostly Reform, none Orthodox—have been ordained rabbis, several serve as cantors and a large number is currently studying for both professions. In the early 1970s a poll conducted by the Union of American Hebrew Congregations revealed that nineteen per cent of all Board members in Reform congregations were women, that five congregations had elected women as their president and twenty-eight had chosen them as vice-president. The numbers of each have increased since then. While far from perfect equality, all this is evidence that contemporary Judaism, especially in the Reform movement, is resolving whatever contradictions afflicted the tradition by moving toward the aims and goals of the women's movement.

Sociologists have long studied the Jewish family with admiration. Few other ethnic groups, if any, can match it in cohesiveness and stability. Rates of divorce, of infidelity, of juvenile delinquency, of child cruelty or abandonment, are demonstrably and impressively lower among Jews. In some degree this has probably been due to extended periods of persecution, when many outlets for diversion and pleasure outside the home were closed to Jews, and they had to compensate for such deprivations with domestic satisfactions.

* The plural of *aliyah,* meaning *ascent* or *going up.* The term is used for going up to the pulpit to participate in the reading of the Torah, also for immigrating into Israel. On the Torah reading, see p. 150f.

It would be an error, however, to attribute the strength and equilibrium of the Jewish family entirely to external pressure. Some of the credit undoubtedly belongs to the wholesome approach to sex, which we have already noted, and some reflects the very high ideals of family behavior which Jewish tradition has recommended through the centuries. Both parents and children were expected to reach for these ideals. Parents were reminded that marital harmony was essential if their offspring were to be secure. The sibling rivalry between Joseph and his brothers was attributed to their father's favoritism for Joseph. According to one chasidic rabbi, "If husband and wife quarrel, they cannot raise good children."

Fathers and mothers were not to forget that their example in deed would provide a more effective lesson than their words. A chasidic rabbi, commenting on the verse in Exodus which reads, "And that you may recount in the hearing of your sons and your sons' sons how I made a mockery of the Egyptians and how I displayed My signs among them—in order that you may know that I am the Lord," said, "It may be remarked that the end of the verse would have seemed more correct if it had been expressed, 'in order that *they* may know that I am the Lord.' But the verse was intentionally worded *you* instead of *they* in order to furnish us a lesson. Recount to your sons the wonders of the Lord, but remember that this will have a beneficent influence upon them only if you yourselves recognize that He is the Lord."

Another chasidic rabbi addressed himself to the same point: "A man asked the Kotzker Rabbi to pray for him in order that his sons might study the Torah diligently. He replied, 'If your sons will see that you are a diligent student, they will imitate you. But if you neglect your own studies and merely wish your sons to study, the result will be that they will do likewise when they grow up. They will neglect the Torah themselves and desire that their sons do the studying.' "

Familial devotion and respect were recognized, however, to be a two-way relationship. Children were obligated too. They were reminded in Proverbs that "a son who deals shamefully and reproachfully will despoil his father and chase away his mother." The same source urged, "Hearken to your father who begot you, and despise not your mother when she is old."

Formal adherence to these admonitions was not enough. The Talmud underscores the fact that the spirit of one's actions toward his parents is even more important than the actions themselves. We read that a man who feeds his father on fattened chickens may be treating him abominably, while one who orders his father to do the heavy work of treading the mill may be acting with admirable affection. In the first instance, if the father inquires where the chickens were obtained, the son may impatiently reply: "Eat, old man, eat and be silent!" In the second case the government may have issued a decree that all millers report to the capital at once. The son, fearing that this presages a period of dangerous military duty for all who respond, directs his father to remain at home, doing the relatively safe work there, while exposing himself to the greater risk.

The responsibilities of both parents and children are implicit in the rabbinic comment that father and mother are partners of God in the rearing of their child. God knew that He would be unable to attend to all the needs of every child, so He created parents to act for Him. One rabbi even suggested that parents were entitled to more honor than God. This he deduced, in typical rabbinic style, from two biblical verses. One states: "Honor God with your substance"— which he interpreted to mean that only if one possesses substance is he obliged to honor God. The other verse reads: "Honor your father and your mother." Here there is no qualifying condition; one is to honor his parents regardless of whether or not he has possessions.

The Talmud gives numerous touching examples of filial

loyalty. It relates that the mother of Rabbi Tarfon broke her sandal one day as she walked through a courtyard. To spare her from walking barefoot on the rough stones, Rabbi Tarfon bent down, putting his hands on the pavement ahead of each step. When he later fell ill, his mother asked the other rabbis to pray for him, saying, "Pray for my son Tarfon, for he honors me more than I deserve." They responded, "If he had done a thousand times more for you, he would not have shown half the honor for a parent which is commanded in the law!"

There is also a description in the Talmud of a Gentile whose respect for his mother was all the more remarkable by virtue of the fact that she had apparently become demented. Once, while he was conducting a public meeting, for no reason at all she removed her slipper and hit him in the face. When the slipper fell to the ground, he immediately picked it up for her. On another occasion she tore his robe, hit him on the head and spat in his face, all in the presence of others. He refrained from retaliation in order to spare her shame.

This is but a sampling of the vast, rich literature, both biblical and post-biblical, which sets forth what Judaism has always maintained a family should be. It would be folly to claim that these ideals were fully attained. People are imperfect and Jews are people. Yet the goal, always there, exerted its influence and achieved substantial results.

The attitudes of Christianity and Judaism respectively toward contraception follow logically and inevitably upon their over-all approaches to sex. If intercourse is basically evil, allowable with reluctance only in order to propagate the species, then any attempt to enjoy it while preventing conception must be sinful. Precisely that has been the prevailing attitude of both Protestant and Catholic Christianity. It is only within the past half century that modification has taken place. Today, concurrent with and resultant from their recent shift on sex in general, most Protestant denominations look with favor on birth control. The Catholic attitude is still painfully ambivalent. Only the so-called rhythm method is officially approved by the Church; this means abstinence from intercourse on those days of the menstrual cycle when it is possible for the wife to conceive. This is accepted as a "natural" procedure; all other methods are prohibited as "artificial." Most medical authorities are agreed that, aside from being an unreliable means of planning families, the practice of rhythm imposes unreasonable restraint which can be harmful to the couple and their marital relationship. Some liberal Catholic theologians have publicly approved the use of other birth control methods by their communicants. As recently as 1968, however, the Pope repudiated their stand, insisting that the historic opinion of the church be sustained.

If sexual relations between husband and wife are inherently good, if intercourse is valid as an expression and enrichment of their love, quite apart from the possibility of a pregnancy, then birth control should be permissible. This has been the historic stand of Judaism. Children were considered to be an essential product of marriage. The first positive divine commandment in the Bible is, "Be fertile and increase, fill the earth . . ." The rabbis later commented, "A man is not a complete man if he has no son and daughter." Also, "A man without children is like a piece of wood, which though kindled does not burn or give out light. . . . A man with children eats his bread in joy; a man without children eats it in sadness."

Quite evidently, it was not because children were believed to be unimportant that Judaism approved the practice of birth control. The rabbis decreed that a minimum of two children would fulfill the biblical injunction. The only disagreement was between those who insisted this meant two boys and those who held that a boy and a girl sufficed.

Conceiving and bearing children were thus recognized by

Judaism to be a proper purpose of marriage, but not its only aim. Hebrew scripture had quoted God, explaining His intention to create Eve: "It is not good for man to be alone; I will make a fitting helper for him." On the basis of this biblical reference, one of the greatest of medieval rabbinic commentators gave sexual companionship as a purpose in marriage no less important than producing children. A man and a woman were permitted to marry and to enjoy their sex relations even if it was known in advance that they were incapable of having children. In short, Jewish religious thought accepted sexual intercourse as a proper aspect of marriage on its own account, quite apart from the desire to procreate. Birth control, therefore, was not frowned upon.

Judaism has never made a distinction between so-called natural or artificial methods of birth control. It looks upon mechanical and chemical means of preventing pregnancy as being no more artificial or reprehensible than administering drugs or resorting to surgery for the improvement or protection of health. Orthodox Judaism does prohibit any contraceptive procedure which must be implemented by the male. This it bases on the fact that the command in Genesis to procreate is couched in a masculine imperative form of the Hebrew verb. Now, of course, the matter is entirely academic, since the most effective methods of birth control currently known require the initiative of women.

Rabbinic law permitted a woman to avert pregnancies while experiencing intercourse if she had previously given birth to children who became degenerate or immoral. It even allowed permanent sterilization of a woman who had found the pain of childbirth to be unbearable, In four distinct places the Talmud repeats the following passage: "There are three women who, when experiencing sex relations with their husbands, may (or must) take the precaution of using an absorbent to prevent conception: a minor, a pregnant woman and a woman who is still nursing her baby." The principle conveyed here is that contraception is permissible to safeguard the health either of the prospective mother or that of another child, unborn or born.[8]

This principle was temporarily in abeyance during the Middle Ages when persecution, expulsion, massacre, and disease conspired to reduce the Jewish population of the world drastically. At a time when the most urgent need was for survival, Jewish authorities tended to look askance at the practice of contraception. In our own time the wholesale destruction of Jewish populations during the Nazi rule of Europe has caused some Jews to react similarly. Occasionally an Orthodox Jew voices opposition to birth control which sounds little different from the Catholic point of view. It is my opinion that such individuals act out of understandable concern for Jewish survival, not in response to the teachings of their tradition, a tradition which, under certain circumstances, clearly approves of contraceptive practice.

The problem of abortion is closely related to that of birth control. Here too, the attitude of many Christian sects, especially Roman Catholicism, has been sternly and unequivocally negative. Abortion is considered by such groups as a form of murder. They believe that from the moment of conception the fetus is a human being with a soul. To abort it, therefore, is in their eyes the destruction of human life.

Judaism does not agree with this view. For one thing, our rabbis never considered the fetus to be a *nefesh*, a human with a soul. Until it had been actually born, legally and morally it was thought of as a part of the potential mother's body, as one of her limbs, for example. According to talmudic law, if a *rodef*, a pursuer, threatens my life and the only way I can possibly save myself is to kill him first, I am justified in doing so. In any situation where a continuation of pregnancy would jeopardize the life of a mother, the same principle was applied; the fetus is thought of as a *rodef*; its life is secondary to that of the mother and is to be sacrificed, if necessary, in order to save hers. In the *Mishneh Torah*, his great legal code, Maimonides summarized the matter as follows: " . . . The sages ruled that, when a woman has difficulty giving birth, one may dismember the child in her womb—either with drugs or by surgery—because he is like a pursuer seeking to kill her."

Suppose there is no immediate threat to the mother's life? Here the rabbis are not of a single mind; some are liberal, others strict in judging the matter. Even the strictest, however, agree that if continued pregnancy would cause extreme mental anguish to the mother, so serious as to carry a threat of either suicide or hysteria, abortion is allowed. In 1913 an Orthodox responsum (rabbinic reply to a request for legal judgment) dealt with the specific case of a pregnant woman whose mental health was at stake. It decreed: "Mental health risk has been definitely equated to physical health risk. This woman who is in danger of losing her mental health unless the pregnancy is interrupted would accordingly qualify."

Similarly, if a pregnant woman is anguished over the possibility that delivering another child might harm one already born or that the fetus she carries may prove to be a defective child, most Orthodox rabbinic authorities would uphold her right to abort. Virtually all Conservative and Reform rabbis would agree.

This should not be misinterpreted to mean that Judaism looks lightly upon abortion or would approve it merely for reasons of convenience. We believe that a couple who prefer not to have a child should practice effective contraception rather than abortion. Yet, under special circumstances such as those described above, abortion is permitted.

A word should be added here on the Jewish attitude toward divorce. The dissolution of a marriage is considered a tragedy of the first order. According to the Talmud, "He who puts away the wife of his youth, for him God's very altar weeps." Marriage was not to be undertaken as a casual experiment. In the words of the Talmud, "A man should not marry a woman with the thought in mind that he may divorce her." Yet Judaism has also recognized that so long as we remain fallible, there will be mistakes in the choice of marriage partners. Divorce was therefore always permitted when a marriage had failed and all efforts to repair it proved unavailing.

A poignant and poetic story is told in our tradition concerning a couple who contemplated divorce on the premise in rabbinic law that a husband whose wife has failed to conceive in a decade of marriage may divorce her. When the husband in question decided to avail himself of this possibility, the couple went to Rabbi Simeon ben Yochai to ask for a divorce. The rabbi advised, "As your coming together was with a banquet, so let your separation be with a banquet." At the banquet the wife caused her husband to drink more wine than he could properly tolerate. Before falling asleep he said to her, "Pick out what is most precious to you in my house, and take it with you to your father's house." After he had fallen asleep she bade her servants carry him on his mattress to her father's house. When he awakened in the middle of the night he was astounded and asked why he had been brought there. She replied, "Did you not tell me last night to take what was most precious to me in your house? There is nothing in the world more precious to me than you!" Apparently the rabbis were as eager for happy endings as are we today. They therefore added that the couple returned to Rabbi Simeon, who prayed for them, and eventually they had a son.

The conditions warranting divorce are first stipulated in the Bible: "A man takes a wife and possesses her. She fails to please him because he finds something obnoxious about her, and he writes her a bill of divorcement, hands it to her and sends her away from his house." On this simple foundation, the Talmud built an elaborate structure of divorce law that was added to the simple declaration of Deuteronomy.

For one thing, the right to sue for divorce was extended also to the wife. Under certain circumstances she could petition the court and the judges could pressure her husband to grant the requested separation. Centuries later Maimonides explained and expanded this as follows: "If a woman says, 'My husband is distasteful to me, I cannot live with him,' the court compels the husband to divorce her, because a wife is not a captive."

What circumstances justified a wife's petitioning for a divorce? She could do so if her husband refused to have sexual intercourse with her, if he contracted a loathesome disease which she could not endure, if his occupation contaminated him with an odor she found intolerably offensive, if he treated her cruelly, or prohibited her from visiting her parents, or changed his religion, or was notoriously immoral. A husband could initiate the petition for divorce if his wife was guilty of adultery, insulted him or his father in his presence, was indecent in public, disregarded the ritual laws pertaining to women, or refused him intercourse. If the two agreed mutually to terminate their marriage, no further grounds were required; the court was compelled to grant their request. No matter what the circumstances of their separation, however, the financial protection promised the wife during their wedding ceremony had to be provided.

In Orthodox and Conservative Judaism it is necessary for a couple to obtain a religious as well as a civil divorce. In Reform Judaism the civil decree alone is considered sufficient. In all three branches, provided the divorce is valid, there is no objection to remarriage.

Although we are deferring to a later chapter our discussion of religious ritual in Judaism, perhaps this is the proper place to describe the formal Jewish wedding ceremony.

Ceremonial observance of the occasion commences even

before the wedding day itself. In the more traditional forms of Jewish practice the bride is expected to visit the *mikvah* or ritual bath, where her immersion in water symbolizes an ethical and spiritual cleansing in preparation for her nuptials. Reform Jews and probably most Conservative Jews today no longer observe this custom literally; yet even they should follow the advice of the *Shulchan Aruch*: "It is essential that the groom and bride, upon entering the nuptial ceremony, purify themselves before God, by repenting of their sins, by reviewing all their deeds from the day of their birth to that day, by confessing their sins and beseeching Him, blessed be His name, to grant them pardon, forgiveness and atonement. They should firmly resolve thenceforth to devote themselves to the worship of God, truly and sincerely, and to be holy and pure, and thereafter they should enter under the nuptial canopy and pray unto the Holy One, blessed be His name, that He may make His divine presence rest among them, as the wise, of blessed memory, said: 'The Divine Presence rests between a husband and his wife.' "

The marriage ceremony itself is called *kiddushin*, taken from the same Hebrew root as *kaddish* (the memorial prayer), which signifies sanctity. In detail the ritual varies from group to group, even from rabbi to rabbi within the same group. Generally it commences with the recitation or chanting of seven Hebrew blessings which acknowledge God as the universal source of love and identify the couple with Jewish tradition. Bride and groom drink from either one or two glasses of wine, symbolizing the fact that henceforth they will taste together both the happiness and sorrow of life. As the groom places a ring on the bride's finger, he recites a Hebrew formula which can be translated as follows: "You are hereby consecrated unto me by this ring [as my wife], in accordance with the custom of Moses and of Israel." In traditional ceremonies the ring must be a plain gold band, without engraving or stones. Reform rabbis permit use of whatever ring the bride plans to wear permanently, even if it be adorned.

In many contemporary ceremonies the bride places a ring on her groom's finger too. Sometimes she is asked to repeat the same formula already enunciated by him, but with a change of gender. Sometimes she addresses him instead with the words of *Song of Songs*: "My beloved is mine and I am his."

Usually at the very end of the ceremony the groom breaks a glass with his foot. This custom probably originated in pre-Jewish times, when it was feared that at a moment of supreme happiness people were especially vulnerable to attack by evil spirits. A glass or ceramic vessel was shattered to frighten these spirits away or confuse them into thinking the occasion was one of sorrow, not happiness. As happens so frequently in all modern religions, this probable primitive origin was later camouflaged by a rationale emanating from Jewish tradition itself. Some said the glass was broken as a reminder of the traumatic tragedy which occurred when King Solomon's Temple was destroyed, or of the fragility of life. Others explained the breaking of a glass as a warning to keep one's hilarity under control.

Among Orthodox and Conservative Jews the couple stand beneath a canopy known in Hebrew as a *chupah*. In Reform and sometimes Conservative ceremonies a simulated floral *chupah* is used. During the ceremony Orthodox and Conservative rabbis read a document called the *ketubah*, a form of religious contract in which the groom accepts certain legal obligations and financial responsibilities toward his bride. Reform rabbis generally replace the *ketubah* with a modified and abbreviated marriage certificate.

Thus does Judaism apply its ethical imperatives to sex, love, marriage, and the family.

CHAPTER EIGHT

The Larger Scene

WITHOUT ENTIRELY IGNORING the social fabric, by and large Christianity has placed its major emphasis on the individual. Without entirely ignoring the individual, by and large Judaism has placed its major emphasis on society. In effect, Christianity has said that only by improving the quality and strength of each brick can a better structure be built. Judaism has countered that, while this is true, the over-all design and engineering of the whole also determine the ultimate usefulness of each brick. Christian faith has divided the human enterprise into neat compartments by taking literally the ambiguous statement credited to Jesus: "Render unto Caesar that which is Caesar's, and unto God that which is God's." Judaism's response is: "The earth is the Lord's and the fulness thereof," which means: Caesar and everything he presumes to accomplish belong to the Eternal.

Nearly all the supplications and confessions in our prayer book are phrased in the plural. On the Day of Atonement (*Yom Kippur*) every member of the congregation—whether or not he has been personally guilty—joins in a long litany of contrition, each line of which details a specific sin, commencing with, "For the sin which *we* have sinned . . ." Even the congregant who is in perfect health joins in the prayer, "Heal us, O Lord, and we shall be healed." The person who is incapacitated and therefore cannot attend pub-

lic worship services is advised to recite his private prayers at
the hour when the congregation is meeting. Thus even in
enforced physical isolation he associates himself with the
group.

In the last third of the nineteenth century and the opening
decades of the twentieth, there emerged in American Protestantism a powerful new movement known as the Social
Gospel, a trend which its chief interpreters, Walter Rausch-
enbusch (1861—1918) and Reinhold Niebuhr (1892—1971)
traced directly to a renewed awareness among Protestant
churchmen of the durable and dynamic influence of the
Hebrew prophets. Its aim was to apply the ethical teachings
of Christianity to the practical problems of society. Unfortunately its influence reached only a small proportion of
the Protestant clergy. More recently a movement has
developed in Christian circles to secularize the church. As
paradoxical as this phrase at first sounds, its meaning is
that the message and institutions of religion should be
brought into the most active arenas of life—into the market-
place, the office, the factory, the bank, the slum. No such
development has appeared in the synagogue, because there
has been no need for it. Throughout its history Judaism has
applied itself as forthrightly to the crises of society as to the
ethical dilemmas of the individual.

A reminder of the chief Jewish theological tenets will
show that it could have been no other way. If human beings
are inherently good; if, as God's creative partners, we cannot escape our ethical responsibilities; if more emphasis is
placed on deed than creed and there is no sharp division of
the sacred from the secular, it follows inescapably that the
ethical imperatives of Judaism must be applied to the problems of government, industry, and business no less than to
those of the home. If the churches, too, have moved in this
direction, they have done so because life has become too
complex, too highly organized, for personal ethics alone to

suffice. Not even the most staunchly righteous person in the world can successfully conduct his business affairs on an ethical basis if his industry as a whole is corrupt. Nor can the most conscientious citizen easily maintain his political integrity if the entire system is rife with dishonesty and deceit.

Yet the problem is not a simple one, especially in the United States, with its long-standing principle that church and state should be separated. It would be a destructive violation of that principle to form a political party with principles that coincide with those of any religious denomination or denominations. Also in conflict with that principle would be pressure exerted by religious bodies to extract financial support for their activities from government. Yet this does not preclude the self-financed effort of religious groups to influence governmental policies on matters of ethical import. Admittedly, it may be difficult at times to discriminate between legitimate and harmful religious action; the need is so great, however, that the difficulty must not be permitted to induce inaction.

With this in mind, let us see how Jewish tradition has been applied to the problems and anxieties of society in the past.

Judaism has developed a virtual obsession with the idea of freedom. The Exodus of our ancestors from Egyptian slavery, mentioned more than three hundred times in Hebrew scripture, is clearly the central event in Jewish history, celebrated elaborately each year in the observance of the Passover holiday. As we shall see, Chanukah too is a holiday especially devoted to the theme of freedom. In an era when slaves were held throughout the ancient world in perpetuity, the Bible established a time limit for all Hebrew slaves. After the stipulated term had elapsed, every slave had to be released. If he had married and acquired children during his period of servitude, they were to be emancipated with him. His master, moreover, was enjoined to provide for his elementary needs during the initial period of his freedom. The underlying philosophy was set forth in Leviticus: "For it is to Me that the Israelites are servants; they are My servants, whom I freed from the land of Egypt, I the Lord their God" (Leviticus 25:25).

In this connection there is another instructive contrast between the Mosaic Code and the Code of Hammurabi. The latter provided that a slave who denied his master or sought unsuccessfully to escape was to have an ear amputated as a sign of permanent disgrace. The ethics of Moses retained this procedure with an ironic twist. If a Hebrew slave refused the freedom offered him in compliance with Levitical law, a nail was driven through his ear lobe to mark him as a man who valued freedom too little to avail himself of it!

Jewish sympathies were always with the persecuted, with those who were denied freedom. The rabbis were perceptive enough to note that all the animals declared eligible for use as sacrifices in the Bible were animals which are pursued by others; no aggressive species was acceptable to the Lord. "When you see a wicked man persecuting a wicked man, know that God is with the persecuted. If a righteous man persecute a righteous man, God is with the persecuted. And even when the righteous persecutes the wicked, by the very fact of their persecution, God is still with the persecuted."

A remarkable example of this Jewish concentration on freedom comes from the Roman period. Jews generally were forbidden by the rabbis to attend gladiatorial combat in the Gentile amphitheaters. This was prohibited not only because pagan religious rites were frequently associated with such events, but also because the gladiators, more often than not, were prisoners who had been condemned by Roman courts. In each spectacle a certain number of them were forced to remain in the contest until released by death. The rabbis judged attendance at such an event to be complicity in bloodshed. The only extenuating circumstance was the fact that usually it was left to the spectators to determine which victims or how many were to be spared. A Jew, therefore, was permitted to attend only for the purpose of joining in a public plea for mercy and freedom on behalf of the gladiators. "One who sits in the stadium is guilty of bloodshed. Rabbi Nathan permits it because as a spectator he may shout for mercy and thus save lives. . . ."[1]

Even in the relatively simple type of economy which prevailed in Bibletimes, it was recognized by the ancient Jew that political and spiritual freedom would be impossible without economic freedom. Hebrew scripture is therefore replete with injunctions ordering fairness and justice for the underprivileged. The Fourth Commandment directed that Sabbath rest was to be extended to one's employees, even his slaves. Other biblical passages were even more specific: "You shall not abuse a needy and destitute laborer, whether a fellow countryman or a non-citizen in your communities. You must pay him his wages on the same day, before the sun sets, for he is needy and urgently depends on it." . . . "When you make a loan of any sort to your neighbor, you must not enter his house to seize his pledge. You must remain outside, while the man to whom you made the loan brings the pledge out to you. If he is a needy man, you shall not go to sleep in his pledge; you must return the pledge to him at sundown, that he may sleep in his cloth and bless you; and it will be to your merit before the Lord your God."

This theme was reiterated time and again by the major prophets. Jeremiah's words were typical:

Woe unto him that builds his house by unrighteousness,
And his chambers by injustice;
That uses his fellow's services without wages,
And gives him not his hire;
That says: "I will build me a wide house
And spacious chambers,"

And cuts out windows for himself,
And it is ceiled with cedar, and painted with vermillion.
Shall you reign, because you strive to excel in cedar?
Did not your father eat and drink and do justice
   and righteousness?
Then it was well with him.
He judged the cause of the poor and needy;
Then it was well.
"Is not this to know Me?" saith the Lord.

Amos spoke on the same theme:

Hear this, O ye that would swallow the needy,
And destroy the poor of the land,
Saying: "When will the new moon be gone,
   that we may sell grain?
And the Sabbath, that we may sell corn?"
Making the Ephah small, and the shekel great,
And falsifying the balances of deceit;
"That we may buy the poor for silver,
And the needy for a pair of shoes. . . ."

The language is archaic, and the economy was simpler and thus easier to control. But the prophet here was excoriating the businessmen of his time for practices which are lamentably still all too common: using false measures and weights, charging exorbitant prices, reaping unjustifiably large profits, and selling defective goods.[2]

Judaism has never condemned wealth as such, or threatened that the rich would have less chance of achieving eternal reward than the poor. It repudiated the attitude toward wealth attributed to Jesus: "Woe unto you that are rich, for ye have received your consolation; and woe unto you that are filled, for ye shall hunger." Or again: "It is easier for a camel to go through the eye of a needle than for a rich man to enter into the kingdom of heaven." Or also: "How hardly shall they that have riches enter into the Kingdom of God!" (Mark 10:23-25). Judaism asks only two questions of the wealthy: did you earn your money justly; and, are you using it generously? An affirmative answer to the second query is no excuse for a negative response to the first. The Midrash stipulates: "If a person steals with one hand, and gives charity with the other, he will not be acquitted in the hereafter."

It would have been atypical for Judaism to call for honest business practices in general and not provide specific examples. Even the original biblical injunction borders on the specific: "You must have completely honest weights and completely honest measures . . . For everyone . . . who deals dishonestly is abhorrent to the Lord your God." Commenting on this and similar instructions, the writers of the Talmud left no room for misinterpretation or doubt: "The shopkeeper must wipe his measures twice a week, his weights once a week and his scales after every weighing." The merchant is enjoined from keeping false measures on his property even though he may not intend to use them; someone else may inadvertently do so.

Prices too came under talmudic supervision. Reb Saphra is held up as an example. Once, when he had wine to sell, a customer came to offer him a certain price. Because Reb Saphra was in the midst of praying and knew that it was forbidden to interrupt one's prayers for conversation, he did not respond. Thinking that silence meant dissatisfaction with the proffered price, the customer immediately named a higher figure. When Reb Saphra had completed his prayers he said, "I decided in my heart to sell you the wine at the first price you mentioned, therefore I cannot accept your higher bid."

The following selection from the *Shulchan Aruch** sounds almost as if it had been drafted with the modern advertising and packaging industries in mind: "One must be most careful not to cheat one's neighbor, whether he is a seller or a buyer, a laborer or a customer. If one has something to sell, he is forbidden to make it look better than it

---

* Sixteenth-century compendium of rabbinic law.

really is, in order to deceive the customer. It is also forbidden to paint over old utensils to make them appear new; and all similar devices are prohibited. It is likewise forbidden to mix a little bad food with plenty of good food or inferior wine with superior wine, and to sell the same as though they were high quality."

Another business abuse, severely castigated by Isaiah, was the concentration of wealth in such a way as to cause injustice to the poor. Though business monopolies in biblical times were not remotely like those of today, the prophet foresaw the danger of condoning them. Therefore he cried out:

> Woe unto them that join house to house,
> That lay field to field,
> Till there be no room, and ye be made to dwell
> Alone in the midst of the land!

The sympathies of the rabbis were usually with the laborers, whom they recognized to be the disadvantaged segment of the population. There is even one account in the Talmud of a strike by skilled bakers and chemists, who won substantial wage increases from the temple authorities because their work could not be duplicated by strikebreakers.[3] Despite this tendency to favor the weaker elements of the economy, Judaism insisted that they too must measure up to standards of equity and justice. In the Midrash, for example, we read of a rabbi who earned his living as a construction worker. There was nothing unusual in this; only in relatively modern times has the rabbinate become a full-time paid profession. One day when the rabbi was working on a house a man came to ask him a question regarding talmudic law. From his scaffold he replied, "I cannot go down [to answer]. I was hired by the day and my time belongs to my employer."

Even the problem of moonlighting was anticipated by the Talmud: "The worker is not permitted to work at night and then to hire himself out again during the day. He also should not go hungry or afflict himself because this is stealing the work of the employer."

Every reason compelling the Jew to measure his business practices by the plumb line of ethics directed him to high standards in his political life as well. The prophets were scrupulous in criticizing their kings for both personal immorality and unethical public policy. The classic example is Nathan's reproaching King David after the monarch had conspired to have Uriah killed in battle so that the king could marry the widow, with whom he had already committed adultery. Nathan disguised his mission by relating a parable about a rich man who expropriated the lamb of a poor man. David declared in outrage that an injustice had been perpetrated and the guilty man should be punished. "As the Lord liveth, the man that hath done this thing shall surely die!" Whereupon the prophet Nathan pointed directly to the king and declared: "You are the man!"

The prophets criticized foreign as well as domestic policy. Isaiah, for example, lived in a time of intense militarism not unlike our own. Egypt and Assyria were struggling for power in the Mediterranean world, much as Russia and the United States are doing on a larger stage today. Little Palestine was located precariously between the competing giants. When King Hezekiah proposed a military alliance with Egypt, Isaiah left no room for doubt about where he stood:

> Woe to them that go down to Egypt for help
> And rely on horses,
> And trust in chariots, because they are many,
> And in horsemen, because they are exceedingly
>   mighty;
> But they look not to the Holy One of Israel,
> Neither seek the Lord . . .
> Now the Egyptians are men, and not God,

> And their horses flesh, and not spirit;
> So when the Lord shall stretch out His hand,
> Both he that helps shall stumble,
> And he that is helped shall fall,
> And they all shall perish together.

One can easily imagine how the super-patriots of the time felt about Isaiah, and what they said of him.

The prophets were not in every instance devotees of non-violence. They emphasized that physical strength could avail only if it was allied with moral righteousness. Zechariah spoke for all of them when he declared:

> "Not by might, nor by power
> But by My spirit,"
> Saith the Lord of hosts.

This brings us, in our inventory of Judaism's public ethics, to the prophetic passion for peace. With the possible exception of freedom, no other ideal ranked so high in the Jewish hierarchy of value. Nor was the Jew's concentration on peace motivated merely by practical or political considerations. It emerged from his universalism, his profound conviction that all men were equally created in the divine image. Adam, construed to be the ancestor of all men, not just of Jews, was said by Jewish tradition to have been created from multicolored dust, gathered from the remotest corners of earth. No person, therefore, would ever be able to boast of nobler ancestry than another Talmudic doctrine asserted that the righteous of *all* nations will share in the world to come.

Two expressions of this universalism are especially cherished by Jews: "I call heaven and earth to witness that whether one be Gentile or Jew, man or woman, slave or free, the Divine Spirit rests on each in accordance with his deeds."[4] And, from the same rabbinic document: "We are obligated to feed non-Jews residing among us even as we feed Jews; we are obligated to visit their sick even as we visit the Jewish sick; we are obligated to attend to the burial of their dead even as we attend to the burial of Jewish dead."[5]

Such universalism impelled the rabbinic directive: "Be of the disciples of Aaron, seeking peace and pursuing it." It was not enough merely to yearn for peace; one had to follow a course of action in his personal and social life which, together with similar efforts on the part of others, would produce peace.

It is profoundly significant that the Hebrew word for both "hello" and "goodbye" is *shalom*, meaning peace. *Shalom* means more than just the absence of conflict. It connotes a sense of wholeness, of completeness, which can be achieved only through the attainment of righteousness and justice. The rabbis said that King David was not allowed to build the Temple in Jerusalem because he had been a man of war; the privilege of constructing the Temple was reserved for his son, Solomon, whose very name is derived from *shalom*. In the building of the Temple's altar no metal was permitted, because weapons of war are manufactured from metal. The Talmud even went so far as to forbid the innocent sale of iron to idolaters, lest they subsequently use it to make weapons.[6]

War was, of necessity, a part of early Jewish history. In no other way could nations or peoples establish themselves then or preserve their integrity. But where most other ancient peoples glorified war, the Jews deplored it and promulgated regulations for its humanization and restraint. Even in times of political and military crisis, a bridegroom was exempted from serving in the army for a year after his wedding and those who suffered inordinate fear were released from military service. Deuteronomy ordered that when a city surrendered, its inhabitants were to be spared; even if it resisted, all non-combatants were to be treated with compassion and mercy.

An attacking army was allowed to lay siege only to three sides of a city; the fourth had to be left open as a means of escape. Under no circumstances were armed forces permitted to destroy fruit trees or water springs; these were to be preserved, since they were needed for sustenance. It is no exaggeration to say that if the restrictions imposed on military efforts by the Hebrew Bible were accepted today, it would be utterly impossible to wage war!

Despite the many wars waged during the biblical period, Jewish tradition never evaluated military prowess as a virtue. Students and scholars have been our people's heroes, not warriors and fighters. The holiday of Chanukah commemorates only incidentally the victory of the Maccabees over the Syrian-Greeks in the second century before the Common Era. Its main emphasis is on the cleansing and rededication of the Temple. Jochanan ben Zakkai, the rabbi who established a modest academy of study while Rome laid siege to Jerusalem in the first century, is remembered, though the names of the captains and generals who led the resistance have been forgotten. Rabbi Akiba, the outstanding Jewish spiritual leader of the second century, occupies a position of higher esteem in Jewish history than Bar Cochba, who captained the major revolt against Rome. From the time of Moses to the establishment of modern Israel, Jews have fought with valor and courage—for their own survival and for that of their host nations. But they never exulted in war or exalted it into an ideal. To the contrary, the rabbis declared, "If one sheds blood it is accounted to him as though he diminished the image of God."

Both Isaiah and Micah voiced the Jewish yearning for peace with memorable eloquence. The latter incorporated in his prophetic poetry the entire scope of this Judaic ideal, its universalism as well as its deference and respect for differences among the nations:

And He shall judge between many peoples,

And shall decide concerning mighty nations afar off;
And they shall beat their swords into plowshares,
And their spears into pruning-hooks;
Nation shall not lift up sword against nation,
Neither shall they learn war any more.
But they shall sit every man under his vine and
    under his fig-tree;
And none shall make them afraid;
For the mouth of the Lord of hosts hath spoken.
For let all the peoples walk each one in the name of
    its god,
But we will walk in the name of the Lord our God
    for ever and ever.

The mainstream of Jewish thought never became unalterably pacifistic, as did the Quaker tradition. Yet there was room in it for those Jews who interpreted all war as murder and their religious imperatives as a ban on participation in war. Absolute pacifism and conscientious objection to war have always been legitimate options in Judaism. Within recent years both the Central Conference of American Rabbis [Reform] and the Rabbinical Assembly of America [Conservative] have passed official resolutions affirming the right of conscientious objection by Jews on religious grounds.

To catalogue the social ethics of Judaism in theory is one thing; but it is more impressive by far to observe the degree to which they are actually implemented by Jews today. Even some among us who have quite forgotten the religious origins and motivations of their social ideals have nevertheless continued to implement them. Competent and objective observers have frequently noted the disproportionate participation by Jews in organizations and causes which aim at combatting injustice.

A clear example of this is to be found in Jewish philanthropy. The first federation for joint philanthropic fund raising on a community-wide basis was founded by the Jews

of Boston in 1895. Every coordinated community appeal
established subsequently has followed this pattern. The
generosity of Jewish giving, both for their own causes and
those of the larger community, is a source of wonderment.
A few years ago the University of Michigan Survey Research Center, reporting the results of extensive studies,
disclosed that a higher proportion of Jews than of any other
sub-group in the United States gives to philanthropy. This
is true even when differences of income are discounted.[7]

The social sensitivity of so many Jews accounts for their
extraordinary participation in the development of the trade
union movement in the United States. An interesting phenomenon occurred in the clothing manufacturing industry,
where Jews were prominent both among the employers and
the workers. Not only were they instrumental in organizing
and leading unions, but the owners among them often displayed unusual enlightenment too in recognizing the legitimate demands of their workers. Frequently the owner of a
factory and his workers had emanated from the same kind
of European background, had absorbed the same social
idealism from Jewish tradition. On several dramatic occasions this was a factor of importance in enabling the men's
clothing workers' unions to lend substantial sums of money
to firms which might otherwise have been forced out of
business.[8]

As any group in society moves upward socially and
economically, it tends to become more conservative, responding to what it perceives as its own vested interest.
Although social and economic change of this kind has taken
place in the American Jewish community, Jews as a group—
even the wealthier ones—are far more liberal in their social
opinions and choices than their counterparts among non-
Jews. More of them vote, for example, in support of large
government welfare appropriations, even though such ex-
penditures will increase their own taxes. In part, this may be

due to memories of what they or their fathers endured a generation or two ago as underprivileged workers. It reflects also, however, the perdurable teachings of Judaism about social responsibility.

In the struggle for civil rights too, comparative studies show less prejudice among Jews than among non-Jews. Jews have played a far more significant role than their numbers alone would warrant in all interracial organizations fighting against discrimination and on behalf of democracy. In 1965 a Jewish attorney who had served as national counsel for the Congress of Racial Equality estimated that seventy per cent of the whites involved in the civil rights movement and ninety-five per cent of the white attorneys serving that cause were Jews.[9]

A 1970 survey rated Americans by religious identification on a pro-integration scale ranging from 0 to 7. The Jews questioned scored 5.79, Catholics 4.53, and Protestants 3.96. Those listed under "other religions" averaged 4.54.[10] Whether they are consciously aware of it or not, these Jews are in fact implementing their ancient religious tradition, which evaluated racial and ethnic divergence as an asset, not a liability. The Talmud directs that when a Jew sees an Ethiopian, which means to say, a person with brown or black skin, he should recite this special blessing: "Praised be the Eternal our God . . . who has made a variety of creatures."[9]

Through such ostensibly secular Jewish organizations as the American Jewish Congress, the American Jewish Committee, and the Jewish Labor Committee, the social ethics of traditional Judaism are applied to concrete issues and problems. There is no way to measure the extent to which individual members or leaders of these groups are motivated, consciously or unconsciously, by their previous studies of Judaism.

The influence of Judaism is more directly apparent in the

relatively recent appearance of social action committees in our congregations. In 1968 approximately a thousand such committees in the United States, about equally divided between Reform and Conservative congregations, were attempting to educate the members of their respective congregations on public issues and to stimulate individual and collective action on their part in accordance with the ethical dictates of their faith. When authorized by the congregational board of trustees, these committees may testify or issue statements on pending legislation. More than a few of these groups have sponsored local employment projects for disadvantaged minorities, raised money for clothing and community buildings in the South, testified on legislative bills, and participated in interfaith projects for construction or rehabilitation of slum housing.

Both the Reform and Conservative movements within Judaism assist their local committees through national commissions on social action, consisting of both rabbis and laypeople. These prepare resolutions on social issues for the conventions of their congregational associations, publish materials and plan programs for their local affiliates. The Union of American Hebrew Congregations [Reform] also maintains a Religious Action Center in Washington. Its director arranges for testimony on bills previously approved by the Union, arranges seminars and training sessions for both Jewish and Christian clergy. Thus do modern American Jews deliberately, consciously endeavor to implement the high ideals of their heritage.

There are, alas, some individuals in the American Jewish community who do not participate in these efforts. Either because they are ignorant of tradition, or because they have become corrupted by economic self-interest, they stand opposed to the thrust of Jewishly motivated social ethics. A long and acrimonious debate preceded establishment of the

Religious Action Center by the Union of American Hebrew Congregations. On the final vote, however, more than a thousand delegates approved this action by a margin of eight to one. Every rabbi is confronted by members of his congregation who are indifferent or antagonistic to the work of their social action committee. A primary rabbinic responsibility is to alert modern Jews to the social impact of their ethical tradition and impel them to behave accordingly.

In the State of Israel too we see the practical consequences of Judaism's social ethics. One of the most unusual organizations in the world is the Jewish National Fund, organized in 1901 for the purpose of buying land and planting trees in what was then Palestine. It is extremely doubtful whether Israel could ever have been established without the JNF. Two things are unusual about it: the manner in which its moneys are raised and the purpose for which they are expended. In Jewish homes throughout the world there are small blue-and-white boxes, in which members of the family regularly place coins to support the work of the Jewish National Fund. Few institutions acquire their substance from so wide and democratic a base.

In the expenditure of its resources the Jewish National Fund adheres to the biblical principle that the land really belongs to God, and follows the biblical precedent that in each jubilee year (every fifty years) all property should revert to its original ownership. This practice was designed to prevent huge concentrations of propertied wealth which would, in the course of time, leave the masses of people destitute. Land purchased by the JNF becomes the property of the entire Jewish people, not of any individual or smaller group. It can be leased out to colonies or settlements for the biblical period of forty-nine years. If, during that span of time, strict regulations are observed—including many which aim at achieving social justice for all those residing there—the lease may be renewed. The land thus acquired may never become private property or be used for speculation.

Another manifestation of Jewish social idealism in Israel today is the *kibbutz* or communal settlement. It is a communist society in the human and social sense, *not* politically; actually it is the most purely democratic type of social structure to be found anywhere in the world. Originally no private property was permitted in the *kibbutz*; everything belonged to the group, and the needs of individuals were provided by the group. Through the years most of the *kibbutzim* have modified their original restrictions so that now a measure of private ownership is allowed. The prevailing atmosphere, however, remains communal rather than individual. Each person works for the good of the group and looks to the group to satisfy his personal requirements. Only a small minority of the Israelis today live in *kibbutzim*, yet the idealism of these settlements has permeated much of Israeli society. An unusually large number of government and military leaders have come from the *kibbutzim*.

The policies and attitudes of Israel toward the Arabs—both those within its own borders and those in surrounding countries—are another arena within which the social idealism of Judaism has manifested itself. This we defer for discussion in a later chapter.

We have examined the theological climate of conviction fostered by Judaism and have looked into its code of ethics, both individual and societal. An important and intriguing question remains. Can all this be said in any sense to be exclusively Jewish? If the query refers to any one theological emphasis or ethical insight, probably not. Much of what was originally Jewish has long since entered into the bloodstream of civilization. Other groups, moreover, have sometimes developed trends of thought or value not too unlike one or another of those nurtured by Judaism.

It is still true, however, that most of the approaches we have studied originated in Judaism and have reached the epitome of their development there. It is also true that all of them together form a uniquely organic pattern in Judaism. I may have eyes that resemble my mother's, a mouth which reminds everyone of my father's, a certain restlessness which is parallel to my sister's. But the combination of all my qualities and characteristics in a total personality is uniquely mine. No less is the case with Judaism. Any one of its ingredients may be found in other recipes. The quantity of each, and especially the proportions of their relationship to one another are identifiably and exclusively Jewish. And the possibility of future creative development in the same direction is hinged to the dynamic survival of this one people and of its heritage. To this we shall return in greater detail later.

CHAPTER NINE

To Observe and Do

THERE IS ANOTHER CATEGORY of behavior which merits discussion in our consideration of "What the Jew Does." Like all religions but perhaps more than most, Judaism recommends to its adherents a rich variety of rituals. Before we consider them in detail, it would be well to examine briefly the meaning of ritual in general and its special role in Judaism.

Ritual can be either pathological or wholesome. Psychiatrists speak of certain compulsive acts—like stepping on every sidewalk crack or washing one's hands every half hour during the day—as ritualistic. These are modes of behavior dictated either by some inner distress or by superstitious belief that they can ward off bad fortune or bring good. Some religious rituals may be not too different from these repetitious actions. They are observed by habit only, with no sense of meaning or purpose, and the individual who practices them might be uncomfortable to the point of illness if even one of them were skipped. This kind of ritual no longer has any truly religious meaning.

There is reason to suspect that the need for ritual is inherently part of the life patterns which preceded the appearance of humanity. We know, for example, that certain animals and birds follow fairly sophisticated forms of ritual, especially in connection with mating. Perhaps our more elaborate and meaningful human rituals are the result of an intrinsic tendency in nature.

At its best, ritual in human life is a symbolic expression in motion of attitudes, feelings, or convictions which cannot be fully communicated in words alone. Often without conscious awareness, we employ rituals of a non-religious nature every day of our lives. Shaking hands with a friend is a ritual: it expresses our joy at seeing him again on a level which mere verbal greeting could not attain. A kiss is a ritual; no combination of words can quite communicate the degree of affection conveyed by a kiss. The Christian participant in communion is acting out and reinforcing his relationship to Christ on a level that limitless volumes of words could not achieve. The groom who reverently places a ring on his bride's finger while pronouncing his marriage vows is saying something to himself and her beyond what the same words without ritual could ever indicate.

A given ritual can be performed either as an enriching act or as meaningless rote. One man can shake hands with his best friend in a perfunctory manner, paying no attention to the significance of what he is doing. Another can put into the physical contact of two hands precious depths of friendship. One person can take communion with his mind many miles away; his neighbor at the altar, concentrating on the inner, enduring significance of the ceremony, may rise a nobler and finer individual. The difference can lodge in the ritual itself as well as in what the individual brings to it.

Some rituals which have been retained through inertia are quite beyond the possibility of intelligent acceptance today. At Oxford University in England, for example, the bell in Tom's Tower is tolled 101 times at nine o'clock every night. This practice originated many years ago when the 101 original students of the college had to check in at nine o'clock, and the bell was rung once for each of them. Now, with many more than 101 students enrolled and with no one checking in at night, the old practice is still followed. It would be difficult, if not altogether impossible, to toll the bell in Tom's Tower today in a meaningful manner. Other rituals, however—if observed attentively and intelligently— can strengthen the individual's relationship with Ultimate Reality and with the particular historic group to which he and the ritual belong.

There are three rationales for practicing the rituals of Judaism. Some Jews, mostly Orthodox, do so because they believe such behavior to be literally God's will. Although most of the ceremonial observances of Judaism originated in the Talmud rather than the Bible, tradition relates the two organically. In theory every law or rule set forth in the Talmud is based on Scripture; there is at least one biblical proof text to support every talmudic statement or regulation. Any ritual ordered in that document is therefore presumed by an Orthodox Jew to be of divine origin. Whether from superstitious fear that punishment will follow if he does not obey, or from a more positive sense that he is following the Divine Will, he tries, by maintaining a traditional pattern of observance, to please God.

A second emerges from the definition of ritual given in the opening paragraphs of this chapter. If it is true that we cannot fully express or realize ourselves by verbal means alone, then the poetic symbolism of ritual is a necessary part of human life. Those who practice a maximum of ritual for this reason can also say they are following the will of God, though they would be interpreting these words differently from the first group. In their view what God wills is that man discover as much as possible about the physical and the spiritual laws of nature, then implement what he has discovered in his life. To the extent, then, that meaningful practice of ritual can bring a person closer to the Spiritual Core of reality, can remind him of his relationship to that Core and stimulate him to conduct consistent with the nature of the universe and himself—to that degree he too can interpret his actions as following the will of the Divine.

A third group observes Jewish ritual with no thought of divine sanction. These people see ceremonial observance as following Jewish custom, the singular models of procedure worked out by Jews in the course of their historic development. They practice ritual as a means of identifying themselves more closely with other Jews, both past and present, and of perpetuating cultural patterns they believe to be precious.

Jewish tradition refers to a ritual act as a *mitzvah*, a Hebrew word which is difficult to translate. It connotes some of the meanings of commandment, commitment, responsibility, with additional overtones. It is interesting to note that the same term, *mitzvah*, is used for an ethical act of distinction. The performance of a kindness, for example, or a gift to philanthropy is known as a *mitzvah*. In connection with either meaning, the word always implies something of a divinely imposed duty. Those who implement Jewish ritual purely as folkways do so entirely because of personal choice. Those who practice ritual for either of the first two reasons elaborated above do so because they are convinced that their personal choice ties in with an inescapable obligation, that a Jew must do these things in order most fully to realize himself Jewishly in relationship to his God.

The prophets often expressed their impatience with ritual. In the eighth century B.C.E. Amos, speaking for God, said:

> I hate, I despise your feasts,
> And I take no delight in your religious gatherings.
> Even though you offer Me your burnt-offerings and
> your meal offerings,
> I will not accept them;

And the peace-offerings of your fatted beasts
I will not look upon.

Take away from Me the noise of your hymns;
I will not listen to the melodies of your harps.
But let justice roll down as waters,
And righteousness as an ever-flowing stream!

Two centuries later Isaiah spoke in similar vein, again in the name of the Lord:

Bring no more vain offerings:
Incense is an abomination to Me.
New moons and Sabbaths and the holding of religious
    gatherings—
I cannot endure iniquity along with the solemn
    assembly.
Your New Moons and your appointed festivals
My soul hates;
They have become a burden to Me,
I am weary of bearing them.

At times passages like these have been construed to reflect a total repudiation of religious ritual by the prophets. Careful reading will disclose this interpretation to be in error. They did not object to ritual as such, but rather to meaningless, hypocritical ritual, the practice of perfunctory ceremonies coupled with neglect of ethical obligations. Judaism does not countenance the replacement of ethical behavior by ritual observance; it holds that the latter should be an aid toward attaining moral improvement. An either-or choice is false to the spirit of Judaism.

A rabbinic comment, based on the passage in Numbers which directs Jews to wear a fringe on their garments, helps us understand the relationship between ritual observance and ethical behavior. An ancient rabbi indicated that the sequence of verbs is important in the biblical passage: "You shall *look* upon it, and *remember* all the commands of the Lord, and *do* them!" He explicitly added: "Seeing leads to remembering, and remembering to doing." The most important function of ritual in Judaism is to serve as a reminder of obligations and ideals, as a stimulus toward fulfilling them.

A word should be added here regarding the *taleet*, the prayer shawl worn by Orthodox and Conservative Jews during morning worship. This practice derives from the foregoing biblical command that the ancient Israelites were to wear fringes on their garments. The probable reason is that slaves then wore short robes in order to move freely and quickly to do the bidding of their masters. Free men wore long robes decorated with fringes. Especially when they prayed, Jews were to stand before God in freedom. Similarly, at the Passover Seder the head of the family generally reclines on one or more pillows because this too marked a free man in antiquity.

Unlike the *taleet*, the *kippah* (the skullcap worn by Orthodox and Conservative Jews when engaged in worship or study) has no biblical warrant, nor is it enjoined in the Talmud. It probably originated in Babylonia, where covering one's head was the customary manner of showing deference and respect. Though ordered in neither Bible nor Talmud, the *kippah* is considered essential by both Orthodox and Conservative Jews. In most Reform congregations the individual is free to retain or discard the *kippah*, as he wishes.

Today Jews differ greatly in the degree of their ritual observance. Strictly Orthodox Jews are persuaded that every act of ceremony ordained in Bible or Talmud must be implemented. The only exception is with reference to rituals ordered in connection with the ancient Temple in Jerusalem; because the Temple has not existed for centuries, these rituals need no longer be observed. Otherwise, the Orthodox Jew retains every traditional practice. Reform and Conservative Jews, however, adopt some ancient rituals and reject others. In the earliest development of Reform Judaism there was an unfortunate tendency to minimize the importance of ritual; more recently Reform Jews, too, have come to appreciate the role of ritual in religion.

A curious phenomenon is to be found here. Some Jews do not accept any of the three rationales for observance of ritual, indeed, do not consider themselves religious at all and feel no attraction for Jewish folkways, yet observe select rituals at certain times of the year. They are likely to join their families, for example, at High Holy Day religious services and at the Seder on Passover. Exactly what motivates them is difficult to explain: perhaps unconscious memories, perhaps nostalgia, perhaps family loyalty, perhaps an almost visceral need to identify, perhaps even a certain amount of guilt at their neglect of religious rites the rest of the year.

The two extreme positions with regard to ritual are easy to follow. The Orthodox Jew who observes everything and the alienated Jew who observes nothing face no problem. All others must have criteria by which to select or reject. Most practicing Jews who are not Orthodox retain those rituals which (a) symbolize an ethical ideal or spiritual principle important in Judaism, (b) commemorate a historic event of supreme significance in Jewish history, (c) add aesthetic beauty or warmth to life, and (d) reinforce the bonds of unity among Jews throughout the world. Naturally, individuals will differ in their evaluation of a particular ritual, even when employing the same standards of judgment. Some variance is inevitable, therefore, from person to person and family to family, even among those who agree that observance of ritual is vital.

Judaism is at least as much a tradition of the home as of the synagogue. Hence many of our rituals are intended for home observance within the family. It is possible for the members of a Jewish family who remain at home on Friday night, the beginning of the Sabbath, to be celebrating the occasion as legitimately and meaningfully as others who are in the synagogue at the same time. This assumes, of course, that they would be reciting the proper prayers, chanting the assigned songs, and performing the indicated rituals.

Before turning to examples of Jewish ritual, a few words are in order regarding the Hebrew religious calendar. There is a minor discrepancy in the length of certain holidays as observed by Orthodox and Conservative Jews, on the one hand, and by Reform Jews, on the other, In talmudic times it became customary to add a day to some of the special religious occasions decreed in the Bible. This was done because the beginning of a new month had to be established by the personal witness of those who had seen the new moon and testified to that effect before the Sanhedrin in Jerusalem. Messengers were then dispatched to all outlying Jewish communities. Sometimes they did not reach their destination until after a given holiday had commenced. The addition of the extra day ensured that even if this occurred, the proper time span would nevertheless be observed. Orthodox and Conservative Jews continue the celebration of those supplementary days because they are ordered by the Talmud. Reform Jews do not; because the original reason for lengthening the holidays no longer prevails, the Reform branch of Judaism reverts to the duration prescribed in the Bible. Except for the Jewish New Year, Israelis also follow the biblical schedule.

Our Jewish holidays seem to float back and forth in the civil calendar. This fluctuation of dates is due to the fact that the Hebrew calendar is determined by the moon, making the year some eleven days shorter than the solar year. To prevent utter chaos, with winter holidays occurring in the heat of summer, a leap year was provided in irregular cycle (seven times in each span of nineteen years), a full month being added to bring the two schedules back into reasonable adjustment. A leap year thus propels all Jewish holidays forward about two and a half weeks in the civil calendar, after which they lose time again until the next supplementary month is inserted.

All our special days commence just before sunset and end the next day at starlight. This follows the precedent established in the Creation story: evening is mentioned first at the culmination of each day's creative accomplishment. "And there was evening and there was morning, a first day" (Genesis 1).

A final note on the calendar: For reasons already clarified in Chapter Five, we do not count time from the birth of Jesus. In the Hebrew calendar the greater part of 1977 was numbered as the year 5737; the year 5738 commenced in September. Traditionally these figures are supposed to indicate the number of years since Creation. Though we know today that our earth is very much older than our ancestors calculated, that it has existed for at least six billion years, not just six millennia, we nevertheless continue our people's time-honored practice of designating the Hebrew year according to Jewish tradition.

It is impossible to include here a full résumé of Jewish ceremonial practice, but a description of some ritual patterns can help us appreciate the flavor of the whole. Sabbath Eve is a good place to begin.

The Sabbath, called *Shabbat* in Hebrew, commences at sunset Friday and ends with the appearance of three stars after sundown Saturday. It is ushered in as the mother of each household kindles two or more candles, reciting a Hebrew blessing which praises God for enabling us to attain sanctity in our lives through the performance of this act. The father then holds aloft a cup or glass of wine as he leads the family in reciting or chanting *kiddush*, a prayer of sanctification which expresses gratitude for the special spiritual role our people has played and relates *Shabbat* to the Exodus from Egypt. Then the *motzee* is pronounced, a short prayer thanking God for food. With minor changes of wording these rituals—candles, *kiddush*, and *motzee*—precede dinner in the Jewish home at the inception of all festivals and holidays as well as the Sabbath. It is interesting to reflect, by the way, that the religious usage of wine and bread in Judaism was adapted by Christianity for a quite different purpose in its communion service.

During and after dinner on *Shabbat* the family joins also in singing *zemirot*, songs especially appropriate to the occasion. The family unity so characteristic of Jews is greatly enhanced by the practice of such rituals.

Kiddush is also chanted over a cup of wine as the Sabbath is welcomed in the synagogue. Some congregations have also instituted the kindling of *Shabbat* candles on the pulpit Friday night to enhance the occasion for those who may not have the opportunity to light candles at home. In congregations which hold their Friday *Shabbat* services after sunset, this is a violation of Orthodox law, which prohibits the kindling of a fire as well as writing or riding on the Sabbath.

Parallel to the ceremonies which welcome the Sabbath is a brief service called *Havdallah*, held at its conclusion on Saturday evening. A multicolored, braided candle is lit, the blessing over wine is recited again, and a ceremonial receptacle filled with odorous spices is passed around after recitation of an appropriate blessing. God is thanked for distinguishing the Sabbath from ordinary days, Jews from other peoples, and light from darkness. One of the explanations given for the *Havdallah* candle, with two or more wicks, underscores a Jewish theological emphasis we have already mentioned: this unusual candle represents the intertwining of the secular with the sacred. The mood of *Havdallah* is encompassed in the hope that the *neshamah yetayrah*, the added soul which adorns the Jew's life on the Sabbath, will bless him also during the coming week.

Even more dramatic than the procedure on *Shabbat* as a home observance is the *Seder* ceremony celebrated on the opening nights of Passover (*Pesach*). The entire family gathers for an elaborate pattern of ritual which precedes and follows dinner. Often twenty or more individuals will celebrate together. The service itself is a narrative rehearsal of the Egyptian Exodus. The book from which the entire *Seder* is read is called *Hagaddah*, meaning "telling."

One of the most impressive examples of synagogue rather than home ritual pertains to the Torah, a portion of which is read at the festival, holiday, and *Shabbat* morning services, as well as on Mondays and Thursdays. As far as content alone is concerned, exactly the same words could be read more easily from a printed and bound Bible. Instead, an elaborate ceremony is followed.

The five books of Moses are retained for synagogue use in their ancient form as a parchment scroll, ornamented with a velvet mantle and a breastplate, crown, and reading pointer of silver. At the proper point in the service, the congregation rises as the rabbi opens the Ark, removes the Torah, lifts it, and carries it forward. This is symbolic of the fact that in Judaism sacred scripture belongs to everyone, and that the most important function of the rabbi is to make it accessible to all the people through his teachings. Musical responses are sung while the scroll is undressed and opened. Then members of the congregation are called up either to chant the blessings before and after the reading, or to do the reading itself. When the portion of the week has been completed, the Torah is rewrapped; the congregation rises again as the scroll is replaced in the Ark. Thus are music, tapestry, and motion combined to demonstrate the importance of Torah and learning in Judaism.

A dramatic supplement is added to the foregoing on *Simchat Torah*, the fall holiday which celebrates the giving of the Torah through Moses. All the scrolls are carried from the Ark in a processional around the congregation. Those who are close enough to the aisles reach out as the scroll passes, touching and kissing it, thus indicating the affection and respect they feel for it. On *Simchat Torah* the concluding verses of Deuteronomy are read, completing the annual cycle of readings which had been commenced the previous year. Immediately another scroll is opened; from it the first verses of Genesis are read. Upon finishing his study of Torah, the Jew should not allow even an hour to pass without starting a new cycle.

Let us return now to the High Holy Days, which precede *Simchat Torah* in the autumn. *Rosh Hashanah*, the New Year, and *Yom Kippur*, the Day of Atonement, are the most solemn religious occasions of the year. They and the ten days between them invite every Jew to take scrupulous inventory of his conduct during the preceding year and to make firm resolutions for improvement in the future. On *Yom Kippur* Jews fast for more than twenty-four hours, abstaining from both food and drink in order to concentrate uninterruptedly on their spiritual status. They attend services in the synagogue to usher in *Yom Kippur* in the late afternoon and for all or most of the following day.

On the evening which commences *Yom Kippur*, a special prayer called *Kol Nidray* is chanted in the synagogue. It is sung to a haunting melody and has impressed itself so indelibly on the Jewish consciousness that the entire evening's liturgy has come to be known as the *Kol Nidray* service. The words mean "all the vows." Enemies of the Jewish people have sometimes alleged that *Kol Nidray* is intended to provide the Jew with an easy escape from broken vows. Jewish tradition proves the contrary, for it states quite explicitly that no formula or rite can absolve the

Jew from a vow involving the welfare of others. The purpose
of *Kol Nidray* is to ask forgiveness for unfulfilled vows
made under duress or those which have been rendered void
by circumstances beyond the individual's control. Thus the
prayer stresses the sanctity of vows and the extreme caution
with which they must be made.

Five days after the Day of Atonement the festival of
Sukkot, or booths, commences. It marks the fall harvest
season in Israel and serves for Jews everywhere as an eight-
day expression of gratitude for the yield of the earth.
Tradition-minded Jews build small booths adjacent to their
homes and, weather permitting, eat their meals there
throughout the week. Under modern urban conditions it becomes difficult, often impossible, for an individual family to
construct its own *sukkah,* or booth. Therefore many synagogues now erect large *sukkot* next to their structures; some
families place small model booths inside their homes. The
sukkot are adorned with a variety of freshly picked vege-
tables and fruits.

A final day added to *Sukkot* is *Simchat Torah,* a day of
grateful rejoicing that the Torah is a part of our people's
tradition. We have already described how, on that day, all the
Torah scrolls are removed from the Ark and carried lovingly in a processional around the synagogue.

In late fall or early winter Jews celebrate the *Chanukah*
festival. Like *Sukkot,* it lasts for eight days. Although
Chanukah frequently occurs at about the same date as
Christmas and is the Jews' occasion for gift-giving at that
time of year, the two holidays are similar in no other way.
True, both probably originated in the pre-Jewish and pre-
Christian celebrations of the winter solstice. The lights
which are prominent in each reflect the primitive custom of
building huge bonfires as the days grew ominously shorter,
an effort to cajole the sun into renewing its vigor. On the
first night of *Chanukah* a candle is kindled, and each night
another one is added until on the final night there are eight.

This custom is derived from the legend that when Judah Maccabee, having achieved the military victory which restored religious freedom to his people, proceeded to cleanse and restore the Temple, he found there what appeared to be oil enough to burn only one day in the Everlasting Light. But the oil in fact burned for eight days; hence the length of the holiday and the number of candles to be lighted.

The Talmud records an interesting dispute on the kindling of the *Chanukah* candles. One eminent rabbi proposed that eight candles be lighted the first night, with the number being decreased by one for each succeeding night. A colleague suggested instead the practice of starting with a single candle and increasing the number until all eight would be ablaze on the holiday's final night. That the second alternative prevailed has been interpreted as symbolizing Judaism's optimism. Even in the darkest of circumstances and times, if but a single flame can be kept alive, from it more lights can be illumined until the darkness is finally conquered.

The first special day in late winter or early spring is *Purim*, commemorating the successful efforts of Queen Esther and her kinsman Mordecai to thwart Haman's attempt to destroy all the Jews of Persia. *Purim* symbolizes a perennial trauma in Jewish history. Haman is the prototype of all those who have threatened genocide against the Jewish people, from Pharaoh through Hitler to Nasser. Esther and Mordecai represent those faithful, loyal Jews who have fought oppression in every age, defending their people and faith with determination. *Purim* is a joyous occasion, celebrated with carnivals and laughter. When the Book of Esther, which recounts the story, is read in the synagogue, the children are provided with noise-makers and are encouraged to use them at each mention of Haman's name. To a lesser degree than *Chanukah*, *Purim* too has been traditionally marked by the exchange of gifts.

We have had previous occasion to mention *Pesach* or

Passover, most especially the *Seder* which celebrates it at home. Like many of our holidays, this was a nature festival in origin; it marked the beginning of spring, the season of planting and promise. Later it became also the time to commemorate the Exodus from Egypt, for Judaism has always perceived the Divine both in nature and in its own unique history. Passover, like *Purim*, celebrates more than a specific event which occurred at a finite moment of time. The *Hagaddah* tells us yearly: "Each Jew is obliged to think of himself as if he personally had been freed from Egypt." We are told to celebrate not only our collective emancipations of the past, but also our firm intention to work for the freedom of all oppressed peoples in the present and future.

Shavuot, the Feast of Weeks, comes seven weeks after the first day of Passover. An agricultural occasion has again been transformed into the celebration of history, without completely losing its original character or intent. As a nature holiday, *Shavuot* marks the early season of grain harvest in Israel; as history, it joyously recalls the giving of the Ten Commandments to our ancestors. Those congregations which hold confirmation services generally do so on *Shavuot*.

The most important Jewish religious day of the summer is *Tisha B'Av*, literally, the Ninth Day of the Month of *Av*. A black, gloomy day of fast, it marks the destruction of both the First and Second Temples in ancient Jerusalem. Tradition has also poetically assigned several other historic Jewish tragedies to this day, which is observed in the synagogue with the chanting or reading of Lamentations, believed to have been written by Jeremiah after Solomon's sanctuary had been demolished in the sixth century B.C.E. by the Babylonians.

The full schedule of Jewish holidays did not spring into being in an immediate moment of miraculous revelation. It developed slowly through historic experience, new occasions being added from time to time, new meanings being grafted to older days. We should therefore anticipate the probability of the Jewish calendar's remaining receptive to further remembrances. In coming centuries, if not decades, the anniversaries of such memorable historic events as the Hitler Holocaust and the establishment of the State of Israel will most likely become special days for our people, commemorated with holidays and rituals no less impressive than those we now cherish.

Indeed, such celebrations have already commenced. Two new holidays have been added to the Jewish spring calendar: *Yom Hashoah* marks the ultimate human depravity of the Holocaust; *Yom Ha-atzma-ut* is Israel Independence Day. Neither is in the traditional schedule of Jewish special occasions; both are observed annually by a majority of Jewish congregations throughout the world.

Rituals of various kinds surround crucial events in the life of the individual as well as his celebration of holidays. On the eighth day following birth, for example, the ceremony of circumcision (in Hebrew, *b'reet mee-lah*) is held for every male child. The surgical part of circumcision— removal of the foreskin from the penis—is done in this country now for most male babies of all faiths as a hygienic measure. In Judaism the surgery is accompanied by a religious rite symbolizing the entrance of the child into the covenant which God established with Abraham. The most significant sentence in the ceremony expresses the hope that "as this child enters today into the Covenant of Abraham, so may he enter upon the study of Torah, a gratifying marriage and a life of good deeds."

In Orthodox and Conservative congregations, a public naming prayer is frequently pronounced in the synagogue for a newly born daughter. Many Reform congregations offer parents the option of such a prayer also for infant sons, either in place of or in addition to the naming which accompanies the circumcision ceremony. We have already referred to the fact that a new trend among Conservative and Reform Jews is to hold a religious ceremony analogous to the *breet mee-lah* for the purpose of welcoming infant girls also into the covenant and community of their people.

A Jewish boy celebrates his *Bar Mitzvah* at the age of thirteen. The term itself implies that he is now approaching an age where he can begin to understand and accept his religious responsibilities on his own, not just by parental dictate. For the first time in his life he is called to the pulpit, usually on *Shabbat* morning, to read publicly from the Torah. *Bar Mitzvah* marks a level of achievement in Jewish education and implies a willingness to continue that education. In recent years most Reform and Conservative congregations have also instituted a ceremony for girls called *Bat Mitzvah*, which performs in their lives much the same function as the older ritual for boys. In addition, all Reform and some Conservative congregations hold a group confirmation service for boys and girls together on completion of the tenth grade of religious school.

The Jewish wedding ritual has already been described. The funeral service consists mostly of recited Psalms and concludes with the *kaddish*. Tradition-oriented Jews recite the *kaddish* in the synagogue daily for eleven months following the funeral, thereafter on the annual anniversary of the death, known as the *yahrzeit*.

Mention should be made also of the *mezuzah*, which literally means "doorpost." This is a small metal or wooden case which is attached to the doorposts of many Jewish homes. In it, inscribed on a piece of parchment, are the words of the *Shema* and of the paragraphs immediately following it in Deuteronomy, commencing with,

"You must love the Lord your God with all your heart, with all your soul and with all your might." Referring to the divine laws transmitted to the ancient Israelites by Moses, the final sentence of the first paragraph reads: ". . . inscribe them on the doorposts of your house and on your gates." Like all other symbols and rituals, the *mezuzah* can be used childishly or maturely, foolishly or intelligently. The occasional Jew who affixes one to his doorpost in the hope that it will bring him good luck or protect his household from harm is indulging in sheer superstition. In Jewish tradition the *mezuzah* was never intended to serve such a purpose. It can have two proper meanings for the Jew today: to identify his home to all who approach it as a Jewish home; and, more importantly, to remind him each time he enters that this is an abode in which God's laws, especially His moral injunctions, must be obeyed. To symbolize the latter, the Orthodox Jew touches his hand to his lips, then to the *mezuzah* as he passes it. In recent years, probably in conscious or unconscious imitation of the medals they see on their Catholic friends, some American Jews have begun to wear small ornamental *mezuzot* (plural of *mezuzah*) suspended on chains around their necks. This was not at all its original purpose or usage.

Another ritual observed by Orthodox and some Conservative Jews follows from the first paragraph enclosed in the *mezuzah*, specifically from the words "Bind them as a sign on your hand and let them serve as a symbol on your forehead." In literal fulfillment of this instruction, during weekday morning prayers a small leather box containing the same words as the *mezuzah* is bound by straps to the left arm, palm, and middle finger, and another to the forehead. These are known as *tefileen,* or phylacteries. Reform Jews interpret the order to bind the divine commandments on their heads and hearts poetically, as meaning that they are to be remembered and implemented.

Judaism is a way of life. The duties it enjoins upon its adherents involve both ethics and ritual. To consider oneself a Jew merely by virtue of birth to Jewish parents, or even by accepting an accredited theological climate of conviction, is not enough. In the last analysis, the Jew is what he does.

PART FOUR
WHAT THE JEW WILL BE

CHAPTER TEN

Promise and Threat

BY ALL THE LAWS of normal human experience the Jew-ish people should have vanished from the stage of history long ago. Numerically insignificant at the start, banished from corporate association with its homeland for nearly two thousand years, exposed to fiendish persecution in every century, this people poses a persistent and enduring mystery. In theory Arnold Toynbee, the historian, was right: Jews as an identifiable group should have expired long since, and their culture should be no more than a fossil. Yet life has a way of refuting the cleverest theory, the most impeccable logic. We Jews are still here—and very much alive.

No people has been persecuted so consistently. Pagan Rome despised us because of our stubborn insistence on freedom, Christian Rome because of our equally intransi-gent refusal to adopt the predominant faith. When the Crusaders were frustrated in their effort to wrest the Holy Land from the infidel Moslem, they wreaked vengeance instead on the Jews they encountered en route. When epidemic and plague decimated much of Europe, blame was assigned to Jews and they were massacred without mercy. Half a millennium after these tragedies Russian Czar and German Nazi, in historic sequence, turned on the Jew as a symbol of that human decency which thwarted ambitions to dominate. The Hitler horror which brutally exterminated six million Jews—one third of the world's total at that time—was only the most recent and most fiendish in a long series of similar cataclysms.

There have been others—like the American Indian and Negro—who have suffered as much or more at a particular time and place. Only the Jew has been consistently persecuted in every time and every place.

This is not the place to analyze the causes of anti-Semitism or to recommend cures. But the odds against Jewish survival are as ominous now as in the past, perhaps even more so. The six million victims of the Nazis are gone. About half as many live in the Soviet Union, where the full power of propaganda and government is directed against the practice and survival of the Jewish tradition. Here in the United States danger looms from the opposite direction. It remains to be seen whether a Jewish community that is freer, more affluent, and less restricted than any in previous history will be able to endure in identifiably Jewish manner. The survival of our people and its heritage into the twenty-first century and beyond is dependent upon both external and internal conditions; in part upon the treatment we are accorded by others and no less upon our own inner conviction and determination.

What difference does it make whether or not the Jewish people as such survives? What difference to ourselves and to the world? Part of the answer is a response to Hitler's nearly successful genocide. If for no other reason, Jews must survive in order not to grant Hitler in death the success he was so narrowly prevented from winning in life. Dr. Emil Fackenheim, a Jewish theologian who survived the Nazi epoch in Germany, has written movingly on this point:

Most assuredly no *redeeming* Voice is heard from Auschwitz, or ever will be heard. However, a *com-*

manding Voice is being heard, and has, however faintly, been heard from the start. Religious Jews hear it, and they identify its source. Secularist Jews also hear it, even though perforce they leave it unidentified. At Auschwitz, Jews came face to face with absolute evil. They were and still are singled out by it, but in the midst of it they hear an absolute commandment: *Jews are forbidden to grant posthumous victories to Hitler.* They are commanded to survive as Jews, lest the Jewish people perish. They are commanded to remember the victims of Auschwitz, lest their memory perish. They are forbidden to despair of man and his world, and to escape into either cynicism or other-worldliness, lest they cooperate in delivering the world over to the forces of Auschwitz. Finally, they are forbidden to despair of the God of Israel, lest Judaism perish. A secularist Jew cannot make himself believe by a mere act of will, nor can he be commanded to do so; yet he can perform the commandment of Auschwitz. And a religious Jew who has stayed with his God may be forced into new, possibly revolutionary, relationships with Him. One possibility, however, is wholly unthinkable. A Jew may not respond to Hitler's attempt to destroy Judaism by himself cooperating in its destruction. In ancient times, the unthinkable Jewish sin was idolatry. Today, it is to respond to Hitler by doing his work.[1]

While the most compelling urgency of this challenge is directed at Jews, it has significance for Christians as well. Napoleon is alleged to have said that the treatment afforded by any nation to its Jews is a barometer of that nation's civilization. Similarly, the survival of the Jewish people is a symbolic test of humanity as a whole, an encouragement to every weak, threatened minority. If this numerically miniscule but spiritually crucial people were, God forbid, to vanish, the adrenalin of hope would be disastrously diminished for all humankind.

A further and even more authentic answer emerges from the uniqueness of any group's collective personality and its contribution to civilization. Our concern here is not with the individual man or woman who contributes to the world something of substance which is unrelated to the fact that he or she just happens to be Jewish. There is nothing specifically Jewish about the accomplishments of a great athlete, a political leader, a business tycoon. These individual achievements could continue beyond the demise of Jews as an identifiable group.

Another kind of contribution could not. Groups, like individuals, develop personalities of their own. These personalities—shaped from common historic experiences, memories and aspirations—enable them to express themselves in unique and singular ways. Even when they address themselves to universal values, to ideals they share with others, they do so with their own inimitable emphasis and style.

Freedom, for example, is a value held in common by all advanced civilizations. No other culture, however, commemorates its past devotion to freedom or rededicates itself to the continued pursuit of freedom quite as do we Jews through our Passover holiday and our Seder ceremony. All lovers of freedom gain through our unique celebration of Passover.

A case in point: some years ago the children of our Religious School invited a group of black youngsters and their minister as guests at a demonstration Seder. This was at a time when the struggle for Black Power was emerging into public awareness. The minister was so impressed with the whole Seder experience that he declared his intention to create a Black Haggadah and asked whether I would read it critically for him. I agreed, though I felt in my heart he would never succeed. I was right. No manuscript was ever forthcoming. A Haggadah could be produced only by a people who had experienced the Exodus from Egypt under Moses and had cherished the memory of that event through all the ensuing centuries. Blacks will have to work out their own distinctive celebrations of and rededication to the ideal of freedom. When they do, though such rituals will be uniquely theirs, emerging from their historic experience, the entire civilized world will benefit.

What all this adds up to is that no one can offer mankind exactly what the Jews—or the Americans, Italians, or Greeks—can. We have already mentioned that whatever Judaism has already infused into the bloodstream of civilization is here to stay. This would be so even if the Jewish people disappeared tomorrow. What would be irretrievably lost is the immense reservoir of untapped Jewish creativity.

The analogy of the individual artist is apposite. Mozart died at the age of thirty-five. Nothing short of mass amnesia or nuclear devastation can ever detract from the impressive number of musical compositions he bequeathed the world, but his creative potential had scarcely been spent at the time of his death. No one can estimate how many additional symphonies, concertos, operas, would have been composed by him had he lived another decade. The moment the physical existence of Mozart was abruptly ended, all possibility of further contributions by him ceased. So it is with a people, in this instance the Jewish people. What we have already given the world merely presages what we have within us to give. With us, as with Mozart, the precondition for such giving is physical survival. Hence our disappearance would be a calamity for more than ourselves.

A rabbinic legend illustrating this truth tells of a Jew who approached the prophet Elijah and asked, "I have two great loves in my heart, and I do not know which deserves my greater devotion. One is the Torah, the other the people of Israel. Which of the two is greater?" The prophet responded, "Most people would say the Torah is more

important. I say the holy people of Israel is more important.
For it is of that people that Torah and prophets came to
mankind." There may be an additional, far-reaching, ethical
revolution, another divine revelation within the creative
capacity of the people which has already offered these
achievements to humanity. Later, in our discussion of Israel
and its importance to the whole world, we shall come upon
certain signs of what this future contribution may be.

The matter of inner Jewish intensity, of Jewry's determination to persist, and of a Judaic education adequate
to accomplish that aim is a problem for Jews to face
within and among themselves. Establishment of political
and social conditions which will facilitate Jewish survival
is a subject to be explored elsewhere. There are two matters
regarding Jewish survival, however, which are so closely
connected to the very nature and meaning of Judaism
that they must be treated here. They are, respectively, the
issue of intermarriage and the complex of problems posed
by the existence of Israel as a state.

Historically, Judaism has always opposed intermarriage,
not from any foolish delusion of innate superiority, nor from
fear lest an illusory "racial purity" be diluted, but rather
because of the danger which such marriages posed to
Jewish survival. The first known statement of opposition
to mixed marriage has been attributed to the first Jew,
Abraham. In sending his faithful servant to choose a wife
for Isaac, the patriarch is reported to have said, " . . . I
will make you swear that you will not take a wife for my
son from the daughters of the Canaanites among whom I
dwell, but will go to the land of my birth and get a wife for
my son . . ."

We can only speculate at Abraham's reason for giving
this instruction. There is no need for speculation, however,
when his preference is embodied in law by the Book of

Deuteronomy which explicitly warns the ancient Israelites that, when they reached the land God had promised them and began to live with the other inhabitants of that land, "you shall not intermarry with them: do not give your daughters to their sons or take their daughters for your sons; for they will turn your children away from Me to worship other gods." From the outset it was the danger of group extinction or disappearance which impelled the Jewish people to oppose intermarriage.

The problem appears even more dramatically in the Book of Ezra, a record written immediately after our ancestors had returned to Palestine from Babylonian exile in the sixth century B.C.E. Ezra, one of the two foremost leaders after the return, instituted the practice of gathering the people regularly to hear parts of the Torah read to them. During their half century in Babylonia, the Jews had intermarried on a large scale. Ezra was appalled by the extent of this practice and the degree to which the fears expressed in the Book of Deuteronomy had been fulfilled: the foreign wives were in fact weakening their husbands' ties to Judaism. The threat was so great that Ezra felt it necessary to impose severe restrictions: not only did he forbid further marriages of this kind, he even decreed that those already married were to divorce their non-Jewish wives.

An altogether different approach to the problem is found in the Book of Ruth. Here we read of a lovely Moabite girl who married a Jew, was accepted by his family and people, mourned him when he died, then again married a Jew. In Jewish tradition Ruth is recognized as an ancestress of King David himself. Here we have a far more permissive and accepting attitude toward intermarriage than in the Book of Ezra, yet both are included in the Hebrew Bible.

Why the difference? There are really three answers to this question. First, Ruth represented a single case of mixed marriage, not a wholesale trend which jeopardized the very possibility of Jewish survival. Second, she lived at a time of relative social ease, when the threat to group identity was nothing like that in the anxious, menacing age of Ezra. Third, and undoubtedly most important, Ruth became a Jewess. The union marked an accretion and a strengthening, not a defection or loss. When read carefully and perceptively, the authors of Ezra and Ruth are not so far apart in their evaluations of intermarriage as might at first be supposed.

Together they set a paradigm which has prevailed throughout Jewish history. If the overwhelming majority of Jewish leaders today are opposed to Jews' marrying out of their own group, it is because the setting of our time more closely resembles that of Ezra than of Ruth. This is more than speculation or theory. Research reveals an alarming increase in the rate of intermarriage among American Jews. The rate in Washington, D.C., during the latter 1950s, for example, was 13.1 per cent. Far more signifi cant than the average as such is the fact that among first-generation Jews it amounted to 1.4 per cent, in the second generation 10.2 per cent, in the third generation 17.9 per cent. There are reasons to believe that the over-all figure may be higher in Washington than elsewhere, but few experts doubt that the trend disclosed there prevails everywhere. The longer Jews live in the United States and the more comfortably acculturated they become here, the larger is the likely rate of intermarriage.

This in itself is enough to worry those who are deeply concerned over Jewish survival. Their fears are heightened by the further fact, revealed in this and similar studies, that a substantial majority of the children born of such marriages are never identified as Jews. The Washington study probed this aspect of the matter too. It asked each couple interviewed whether they had told their children they were Jews. This telling alone sufficed; if there were no Jewish practice in the home, no enrollment of the children in any kind of Jewish school, so long as their partly Jewish origin had even been mentioned, the children were classified as Jewishly identified. Even with so lax and attenuated a tie as this, only 30 per cent of the children involved could qualify! Other research undertaken elsewhere indicates that no more than a fourth of the children born to such couples are encouraged to consider themselves Jewish.

As these paragraphs were being drafted the press reported at length on the dramatic story of a Jesuit priest who had left the priesthood to marry. Buried near the end of the story was the significant fact that his father had been a Jew who intermarried with a Catholic and converted to Catholicism after their first child was born. This is only a single case, but it is typical enough of many others to constitute an ominous threat to the Jewish future.

Perhaps a people which is in the majority, or even a substantial minority, can afford to take such risks. Jews in the United States, however, are a diminishing proportion of the population: in 1937, 3.7 per cent, in 1963, 2.9 per cent. It has been reliably estimated that if current trends continue, by the year 2000 we shall be no more than 1.6 per cent of the total American census.

There is more than one cause for this decline. The birth rate among Jews has been lower than among others; there is also some alienation among Jews who marry within the fold; but mixed marriages are so substantial a part of the danger that they cannot be ignored.

Largely for this reason, an overwhelming majority of American rabbis refuse to officiate at the marriage of a non-Jew to a Jew. No Orthodox or Conservative rabbi, and only a minority of Reform rabbis will do so. Indeed, the Central Conference of American Rabbis (Reform) has officially called upon its members to desist from officiating at such ceremonies, though no penalties or sanctions are imposed upon those whose consciences compel them to disagree. Most rabbis feel they would be faithless to their responsibility for Jewish survival were they to solemnize a ceremony which would, in all probability, aid and abet the disappearance of a Jewish family. They will gladly meet with any couple contemplating marriage of this kind, will discuss with them the difficulties and tensions to be faced, will offer any help or advice in their power, but they will not officiate at such a wedding unless the non-Jew first converts to Judaism. It is then no longer a mixed marriage. Those rabbis who are exceptions feel that by agreeing to participate, they may increase the chance of eventual affiliation with the Jewish community.[2]

It is important to recognize that, notwithstanding everything we have said, the attitude of Judaism about mixed marriage is not at all similar to that of the Catholic Church. Though they see important advantages in a religious ceremony, Jews recognize the validity of civil marriages. The husband and wife married by a justice of the peace are not judged to be living in sin, nor are they considered to be illegitimate parents when their children are born. So far as Reform congregations are concerned, they can become members of a synagogue and send their children to the school whether or not conversion has occurred.

What is the attitude of Judaism toward conversion? Except for a brief interval in the past, we have never been a missionary people. Indeed, our own sour experience at the receiving end of such enterprise has disposed us, on the whole, most unfavorably. We have already seen that throughout much of the Middle Ages, Jews were forced to attend church services and to hear sermons aimed at converting them to Christianity. Rabbis frequently were forced into public debate with Christian clergy, debate they could never win. If their arguments proved too effective, they were deemed offensive and the entire Jewish community suffered dire consequences. On many occasions in history the only alternative to persecution, even torture and death, for millions of Jews was conversion to Christianity. Yet with few exceptions most Jews refused the offer; the price—Jewish extinction—was too high. Any people exposed to such transactions might be expected to have a poor opinion of missionary activity.

In recent years some Reform and Conservative Jews have felt that greater effort should be expended in the direction of educating non-Jews about Judaism. It has been suggested that many persons—in quest of a spiritual orientation to life and dissatisfied with the philosophies and theologies of their past—might benefit greatly from Judaism, perhaps even consider conversion. Yet few, even among those thus favorably disposed, would want a crusading missionary policy. Most of them really favor a more vigorous program of public education.

Though it has seldom sought converts, under the proper conditions Judaism has welcomed them. Our rabbis were told to push a prospective convert away with one hand while drawing him close with the other. The motives and intentions of such a person were to be scrutinized carefully. By itself, a desire to marry a Jew was not generally accepted as sufficient; the prospect had to demonstrate also a genuine desire to accept Judaism and live a positive Jewish life. He was reminded that in becoming a Jew he was taking upon himself certain disabilities which he had not suffered in the past. Only when both the candidate and the rabbi were satisfied on these counts was preparation for conversion to Judaism begun.

That preparation consists primarily of study. It will be remembered that, according to the rabbis, "an ignorant person cannot be a pious person." If this was true for one born a Jew, how much more did it apply to one who wished to *become* a Jew? The content of such studies today will vary from group to group, even at times from rabbi to rabbi. In Orthodoxy and to some extent Conservatism, the heaviest curricular concentration will be on home practices and ritual ceremony. Reform Judaism does not neglect this area, but directs the candidate's attention also toward history and theology. In many large cities a number of congregations have combined to offer a unified program of study for those contemplating conversion. Usually an effort is made simultaneously to acquaint the candidate with Jewish life as well as Jewish beliefs. He is expected to attend religious services, participate in a Passover *Seder* if his preparation occurs at that time of year, and involve himself in the secular as well as the strictly religious phases of congregational life.

To be converted by an Orthodox or Conservative rabbi, male candidates must undergo circumcision; both males and females must be immersed in the ritual bath, the *mikvah*. Most Reform rabbis have dispensed with both these requirements, asking only that the convert agree to the circumcision of any male children born to the couple in question. Traditionally, a conversion can be consummated only by three co-officiating rabbis. In Reform circles one rabbi may conduct the ceremony in the presence of two or more Jewish witnesses. The conversion itself is a brief prayer service, often held in a chapel before the opened Ark. The candidate pledges himself to accept Judaism, to live by its practices and teachings, to rear his children Jewishly, and to cast his lot with the Jewish people under all circumstances.

Any reservation or reluctance exhibited by Jewish tradition toward the practice of conversion does not apply in the case of the person who has completed his preparation and has already been converted. He is warmly welcomed and considered in virtually every respect a Jew. The only exception in Jewish law is that such a person could not become a *cohane,* a priest, or a *levi,* a priest's assistant. In modern times this deprivation has no real significance. Jews were divided in biblical days into three major groups: the *cohaneem,* or priests; the *levi-eem,* or Levites, who were priests' helpers; the *Yis-ra-ayleem,* Israelites, who were the masses. These classifications possessed meaning only so long as the Temple functioned in Jerusalem. Though Orthodox Jews still maintain distinctions in such matters as the order in which men are called to read from the Torah, for all practical purposes the matter is academic. In contemporary life the convert suffers no major disadvantage, for even a born Jew who was not descended from *cohaneem* or *levi-eem* can never become one.

The measure in which Jewish law accepts converts is revealed in the reply Maimonides gave a questioner who wanted to know if, as a convert, he should join the congregation in the prayer commencing, "Our God and God of our fathers. . ." The answer was affirmative: once converted, a person is to be considered so fully a Jew that he should act as if his ancestors too had been Jews. The Talmud stipulates, moreover, that a convert is never to be reminded of the time when he was not a Jew, lest he deduce from such reminders that he is not yet fully accepted.

Unfortunately, there are instances from time to time in which Jewish parents are reluctant to accept graciously a son- or daughter-in-law who has converted to Judaism. It is clear that such individuals, though Jewish, do not know the teaching of Judaism. Their behavior is motivated by some emotional quirk, not by Jewish law; often it emerges from unconscious guilt as to their own loyalty and faithfulness toward Judaism. The tradition itself is not ambiguous.

Though concern for Jewish survival is the predominant reason for the opposition of Judaism to mixed marriage, there is a second important reason. Our tradition values the institution of marriage too highly, is concerned too profoundly with the happiness accruing to husband and wife, to overlook the severe disadvantages a mixed couple invite upon themselves and their children. Whether a given couple likes it or not—whether they accept or attempt to deny it—the plain, stubborn, realistic fact is that their chance for happiness and success is very much diminished if they come from different religious or racial backgrounds.

The stage and motion picture screen would have us believe otherwise. A generation and more ago there was *Abie's Irish Rose*, a sentimental melodrama depicting the match between a Jewish man and an Irish-Catholic girl. More recently there was *Guess Who's Coming to Dinner*, a movie portraying the love of a Negro physician for the daughter of a white journalist. The theme of both is that love triumphs, that if two people love each other enough, they will overcome all obstacles to happiness. Would that it were always so!

Every marriage is, to some extent, a gamble. Even where bride and groom have inquired into their compatibility as carefully as possible, even where they are mature and seem well matched, there is always an element of risk when they pronounce their marriage vows. No one can guarantee to any couple that their love will be strong enough to sustain the burdens and tensions they will be called upon to bear. Where husband and wife come from divergent religious or racial backgrounds, they increase the load considerably. In addition to the problems which every marriage must normally be expected to solve, they invite into their lives a surplus of stress. Under the immediate impact of either love or infatuation, there is an almost irresistible temptation for such couples to assume they will be the exceptions which prove the rule. Many a divorce, many an unhappy home which avoids divorce, attests to the contrary.

There is, in addition, reason to suspect inner imbalance on the part of one or both partners when mixed marriage is being contemplated. The forces drawing two persons of opposite sex to each other may be wholesome or neurotic. The probability of the latter is greater in mixed matches. We do not mean to imply that this is always the case. Theory and study have established, however, that the choice of an unsuitable marriage partner can be motivated by rebellion against one's parents or against an onerous or distasteful tradition. It can also issue from the unconscious need of an individual—realistically or in fantasy—to improve his social status. The wider the discrepancy in background between two persons—socially, economically, culturally, and especially religiously or racially—the more reason there is to suspect such unhealthy motivation.

The findings of several research projects confirm this suspicion. One suggests that the unstable and rebellious are two personality types in minority groups which are particularly prone to undertake a mixed marriage. Another concludes that among those marrying outside their original religious or racial group will be a disproportionate number who are "unorganized or demoralized, . . . detached, . . . rebellious,. . . marginal." In short, the traits of personality which lead to participation in mixed marriages are the very ones which do not augur well for marital happiness or success.

Jews are not the only ones to oppose intermarriage; most Christian religious bodies do too. The Methodist, Lutheran, and Catholic churches are among those who have made strong public statements along this line. These denominations need not fear assimilation or the disappearance of their tradition, but they too are aware that the prognosis for success in instances of intermarriage is alarmingly lower than when marriage takes place within a given group.

Much statistical evidence confirms this conviction. In cases of religiously mixed marriage, divorce occurs three to four times more frequently than the norm. In an early scientific study of marriage Burgess and Cottrell concluded that a husband and wife who come from the same religious origins had eleven times the chance for happiness of an intermarried couple.[3] A study released by the American Youth Commission revealed the following percentages of young people who came from broken homes:

Both parents Jewish	4.6%
Both parents Catholic	6.4%
Both parents Protestant	6.8%
Parents from mixed religions	15.2%
Parents with no religion	16.7%

Those who assume there will be no trouble because neither partner to the match is strongly attached to his religious tradition make two mistakes. First, they overlook the very real possibility that later in life, especially after the arrival of children, one or both of them may feel quite differently about religion. Second, they foreclose from the outset the important role religion can play in cementing their relationship, in enriching their marriage. I am not the only rabbi who has sat with the heartbroken father of a boy whose thirteenth birthday was approaching, witnessing his tears at the thought that because of intermarriage and previous indifference, his son would be the first in many generations not to celebrate a Bar Mitzvah.

Children are often the gravest complication and the most painfully damaged victims of mixed marriages. In traditional Jewish law the child of an intermarriage automatically follows the religion of its mother. With or without conversion of a Christian husband to Judaism, whether or not the child is ever enrolled in a Jewish school, so long as his mother was Jewish, Orthodox and Conservative

Jews accept him too as a Jew. Reform Judaism departs from tradition in this respect. Regardless of which partner to the marriage was Jewish, children who are enrolled in a Jewish school and remain in it through the confirmation ceremony are considered to be Jews. This technical distinction however, does not obviate in any way the anxieties and traumas often suffered by such children.

A child has no deeper need than to feel that he belongs. If he lives in a religiously divided home, his chance of experiencing such security is decreased. At best, he may be haunted by corrosive doubt. At worst, he may bitterly resent the choice his parents have made for him or become the pathetic rope in an emotional tug of war between competing parents or grandparents. The prospects are not pleasant to contemplate.

It is sometimes said that a religiously or racially mixed marriage poses so many problems only in our kind of society; in other parts of the world where less pressure is brought to bear on a couple by the culture, we are told, the possibility of happy adjustment is greater. There may be a measure of truth in this, but the fact of the matter is that most couples contemplating mixed marriage will have to live in our kind of society and culture. The fact is also that the success of a marriage is determined more by internal than by external influences. Basic compatibility is essential no matter what the tone of the larger culture. Consequently, religion is a factor of immense importance in marriage. When it becomes a bone of contention, or a mined no-man's-land to be avoided at the risk of precipitating an explosion, or a treasure trove permanently closed by prior agreement, the possibility of a thoroughly happy marriage is not enhanced.

Because it is concerned with its own survival and, at the same time, cares about happy marriages and families, Judaism has in the past opposed mixed marriage. When

a Jew and a non-Jew find that they are in love, the same
reasons prompt most Jewish authorities today to urge
that conversion to Judaism be given careful consideration.
To be sure, no one has a right to play God in the lives of
others. It is never easy to reconcile the requirements of
the group and the happiness of the individual when they
clash, but the conflict is not always what it superficially
appears to be. Often the happiness which entices the individual is deceptive. It is quite possible that the age-old
experience and wisdom of the group have something to
contribute to the long-range welfare of its individual members.

CHAPTER ELEVEN

If I Forget Thee ...

NOT ALL AMERICAN JEWS are agreed in their attitudes toward the State of Israel. In our opening pages, in attempting to define a Jew, we came across two individuals who strongly disapproved its existence. They represent, however, atypical exceptions. In overwhelming numbers, the Jews of this country—indeed, of the entire world—feel bonds of the most intense attachment to Israel.

Whatever the differences of degree or tone, for virtually all American Jews Israel's several wars have produced a trauma of incredible proportion, revealing unsuspected depths of loyalty and fear, untapped reservoirs of affiliation and faith. The Israelis themselves, including their diplomatic representatives in this country, have been astounded at the reaction and response of the American Jewish community.

Israel's precarious plight has also disclosed an incredible breakdown of communication between the religious leaderships of Judaism and Christianity. The Six Day War of 1967 highlighted a malady which continues to infect interfaith relationships in the United States. During the month of May and early June, when every hour brought an ugly new Arab threat to exterminate the Jews of Israel—to take up where Hitler left off, completing his obscene final solution—neither the National Council of Churches nor the

National Conference of Catholic Bishops uttered a single word in condemnation of the Arabs' vow to destroy Israel or in defense of Israel's right to survive, nor did any other major Christian body in the United States.

After the brief but decisive conflict had ended in victory for the Israelis, some Christian spokesmen reacted with nothing less than blatant anti-Semitism, almost as if the Israelis had let them down by winning a war they were supposed to lose. Dr. James Kelso, once a moderator of the United Presbyterian Church, branded Israel the sole culprit in the Middle East, referring to the recently concluded conflict as "this third Jewish war against the Arabs" and assessing the victory as perhaps the most serious setback to Christendom since the fall of Constantinople in 1453. Dr. Henry P. Van Dusen, well-known leader of liberal American Protestantism and President of Union Theological Seminary for almost two decades, wrote a letter to *The New York Times* (June 26, 1967) in which he said, "All persons who seek to view the Middle East problem with honesty and objectivity stand aghast at Israel's onslaught, the most violent, ruthless (and successful) aggression since Hitler's blitzkrieg across Western Europe in the summer of 1940, aiming not at victory but at annihilation."

Dr. A. Roy Eckardt, prominent Protestant leader, responded with quiet fury to this accusation of Israel by his former teacher, calling it an "unspeakable distortion of the facts." He condemned Van Dusen for stooping "to call black white, to label as 'aggressors' the targets of aggression, and to identify as 'annihilationists' those who barely escaped being annihilated by a foe pledged to turning them into corpses, and who, after their own victory, now manifest an almost incredible restraint and readiness to deal righteously with their would-be slayers."

Though a few solitary Christian voices here or there echoed Eckardt's indignation, the mass of official opinion in Christendom either took refuge in silence or expressed concern only for the Arab refugees or pleaded for action by a United Nations which had already shown itself to be hopelessly biased against Israel and impotent against Arab aggression. To this day there has been no collective Christian protest against the treatment of Jews in Arab lands, who suffer discrimination which surpasses anything the Arabs are alleged to have experienced at the hand of Israel.

The number of Jewish refugees from Arab lands who have been settled in Israel just about balances the total of Arabs who have left their former homes in Israel. Those Jews who have been less fortunate, who have had to remain in Arab countries, have suffered tremendously. In the spring of 1969 a British Broadcasting Corporation news crew was working in Syria and Iraq shortly after the public hanging by Iraqi authorities of nine Jews and five non-Jews on charges of spying for Israel. Notes were passed to them surreptitiously by fearful Jews. One message, penned in Baghdad, said, "About fifty [Jews] are still detained including four women. Most of them are not allowed to contact their parents or anyone else, even a lawyer. Nobody knows where they are."

Another note ended, "Please, we need so much to leave Iraq. Save us." A Jew in Damascus scribbled on a piece of paper handed to the British telecasters, "We are living in hell."[1] Christian religious leaders who have protested vociferously about the plight of Arab refugees have remained strangely silent about the abuse of Jews who have lived for many centuries in Arab lands.

Father Edward H. Flannery, executive secretary of the U.S. Catholic Bishops' Secretariat for Christian-Jewish Relations, has stated that in the Christian community "there is a generalized indifference to the welfare of Israel that shades off into hostility toward Israel."[2] While there has been some noteworthy improvement, hostility toward Israel continues in Christian circles to this day.

Some American Jewish leaders are so disillusioned and

crushed by these attitudes that they have recommended terminating all interfaith dialogue. They feel that if decades of ecumenical exchange have failed so miserably to interpret Jewish aspirations in times of crisis, no useful purpose could be achieved by continuing the effort. A majority of rabbinic and lay leaders do not feel this way but are convinced that what is needed is more rather than less interdenominational conversation, not only more in quantity, but also at substantially greater depth. Certainly one of the first goals of such contacts must be an attempt to understand why so much of the Christian reaction to Israel has been negative.

The explanation lies, at least in part, in the failure of Christians to define Judaism accurately. They have seen it as strictly a religious denomination like their own, as an ecclesia, a church. The extra-religious components of Judaism, discussed at length in Chapter One, have never really penetrated the consciousness of most non-Jews. The uniqueness of the Jewish group, the fact that it defies definition by any of the customary sociological labels, has baffled them—if, indeed, they were even aware of it. Despite maps of ancient Palestine on the walls of Christian Sunday School rooms, moreover, the role of a particular land in Jewish history and theology has almost entirely escaped them. Many Christians saw the events of June 1967 and October 1973 only in political terms. They did not realize that for most Jews, these were crises of major religious proportion too.

Too few Christians have understood that the relationship of the Jewish people to the Holy Land was from the beginning a condition of their covenant with God. "And the Lord said to Abram, after Lot had parted from him, 'Raise your eyes and look out from where you are, to the north and south, to the east and west, for I give all the land that you see to you and your offspring forever. . . .

Up, walk about the land, through its length and its breadth, for I give it to you.' "

The promise was repeated through Moses. Again and again the people were reminded that their wanderings in the wilderness and the entire structure of ethics and law with which they were being inculcated were preparation for their future tenancy of the Promised Land. "Be careful, then, to do as the Lord your God has commanded you . . . so that you may thrive and that it may go well with you, and that you may long endure in the land you are to occupy. . . . And this is the instruction—the laws and the norms—that the Lord your God has commanded [me] to impart to you, to be observed in the land which you are about to cross into and occupy. . . . When the Lord your God brings you into the land which He swore to your fathers, Abraham, Isaac, and Jacob to give you . . ."

After the ancient Israelites had been banished into Babylonian exile, they yearned ceaselessly to return to the land they loved. Their prophets continually reminded them that God's promise still prevailed. The second Isaiah was typical:

> Fear not, for I am with you;
> I will bring your seed from the east,
> And gather you from the west;
> I will say to the north: "Give up,"
> And to the south: "Keep not back,
> Bring My sons from far,
> And My daughters from the end of the earth. . . ."

Or again:

> And the ransomed of the Lord shall return,
> And come with singing unto Zion,
> And everlasting joy shall be upon their heads. . . .

For nearly nineteen centuries as the Jew wandered from country to country, from continent to continent, he carried with him a portable spiritual homeland which he cherished

lovingly in his heart and prayers. During the long night
of their expulsion from Palestine, in an almost quixotic
way Jews everywhere lived more by the calendar of that
precious little land than of the country in which they re-
sided. They prayed for rain and dew in the season when
Palestine needed them most. At winter's most frigid peak
in Moscow or Warsaw or Duluth, they celebrated the
New Year of the Trees because it was time for early spring
planting in Palestine. A medieval mystic proclaimed that
Israel, the Torah, and God are one. Though he used the
first of these terms in its demographic sense, referring
to the people of Israel, his statement is no less true if Israel
is construed to designate the land and the state.

Few writers expressed the significance of Israel more
perceptively or eloquently than Maurice Samuel, an eloquent Jewish spokesman of our time:

> It is written that the story began with Abraham, who
> made a covenant with God, and in the covenant was
> pledged to found a people that would serve the world,
> be a blessing to the families of the earth. It is written
> that the covenant was renewed to the people, Abra-
> ham's descendants, gathered at the foot of Sinai; and
> it is written, again, that the fulfillment of the pledge
> was linked forever with the land of Israel. If this is only
> legend, we are faced with a truth as wonderful as any
> legend, for we must ask: At what point, and for what
> reasons, did our remote forefathers take upon them-
> selves so burdensome and uncalled-for a destiny,
> fastening it upon themselves retroactively in the name
> of mythical ancestors? Whether its origin be legend
> or literal truth, the Jews have struggled with that des-
> tiny for more than three thousand years. At times they
> seemed ready to relinquish it, but always, perversely,
> obstinately, they resumed it, and always the pledge was
> there, to serve the world. The creation of the State of
> Israel is one more resumption of the destiny.[3]

In biblical times the indissoluble unity of people, deity,

and land, as recognized by both Jew and non-Jew, was aptly illustrated by the story of Naaman and Elisha, narrated in the Second Book of Kings. The Aramean general had come to the prophet to be healed of his leprosy. Elisha bade him bathe seven times in the Jordan River. Naaman, looking upon such advice as sheer superstition, did so reluctantly; but behold, he was cured! Before departing, he asked the prophet for a gift: two mule loads of Palestinian earth to take back with him to his own country, that henceforth he might stand on the soil of Israel while worshiping the God of Israel who had effected his cure. In this way he reflected the feeling of Jews through the centuries toward the land of their origin.

Forgive me a personal illustration. My grandfather was an eminent Orthodox rabbi who, on his death, was buried with a small sack of earth from Palestine placed under his head. This religious rite has long been the practice of observant Jews, wherever they have lived, attesting to the affection of the Jewish people for the land in which their faith was born. For the Jew, his faith in God, his devotion to Jewish learning, his attachment to Jewish ethical values, and his love for the Land of Israel have all been indivisible aspects of Judaism. No one who fails to understand this can hope to appreciate how Jews everywhere feel about Israel.

Nor can such a person realize what Jerusalem means to Judaism and Jews. The Holy City is mentioned in the Hebrew Bible no fewer than 669 times. The rabbis declared, "Ten measures of beauty descended upon the world; Jerusalem took nine and the rest of the world took one." Orthodox Jews pray three times daily for the peace and rebuilding of Jerusalem. For centuries, religious Jews have concluded their Passover *Seder* as well as their services on *Yom Kippur* with the Hebrew words "*Lashana haba-ah biru-sha-layeem*—Next year in Jerusalem." Most revealing of all is the strange and wondrous anomaly that even Jews who already live in Jerusalem repeat this hope twice yearly. A prayer for the rebuilding of Jerusalem and the restoration of Zion is included in every traditional Jewish wedding ceremony. Our tradition speaks of two Jerusalems: *Yerushalayeem shel matah*, the earthly city, and *Yerushalayeem shel ma-alah*, its heavenly counterpart. A song composed in 1967, first popularized during the June war, has become almost a second national anthem for the Israelis. It is called *Yerushalayeem shel zahav*, "Golden Jerusalem."

It has been said that Jerusalem is a city sacred to three faiths. So it is. Yet no people has ever possessed such precious ties to Jerusalem as the Jews. No other faith mourns its dispossession from Jerusalem as we Jews do on *Tisha B'Av*. No other daily liturgy prays for a return to Jerusalem. Certain sites in the city are sacred to Christendom, but not the entire area. The Dome of the Rock is only the third holiest place in the world for Islam. (Mecca and Medina are the other two.) For Jews, every step and stone of the entire land, especially of Jerusalem, is sacred.

This indissoluble link to the Land of Israel, both spiritually and physically, is as strong today as it has been for centuries. During the war of 1948, unleashed by seven Arab nations at the instant of Israel's birth, there was only one access to Jerusalem—a winding, steeply ascending road to the mountaintop city. The sacrifices made to traverse that road and save the ambushed Jews of Jerusalem were heroic and epic beyond description. Convoy after convoy was destroyed by Arab soldiers, firing with impunity from the ominous heights on both sides. What is now called the Road of Valor is still lined with the burned-out ruins of half-tracks and trucks. Many hundreds of brave young Jews were killed in order that the Holy City might be liberated. This defense of Jerusalem stemmed from more than just military or nationalistic fervor. On the side of each truck attempting to carry supplies to the city were inscribed the unforgettable words of Psalm 137: "If I forget thee, O Jerusalem, let my right hand wither. Let my tongue cling to the roof of my mouth if I set not Jerusalem above my chiefest joy!"

The insistence by Israel that Jerusalem must be its capital is thus more than a matter of sheer stubbornness. Both before and after the outbreak of hostilities in 1967, the Israel Government assured King Hussein of Jordan that if he would desist from attacking the city, no military action would be taken against him. Hussein refused. After he had initiated combat and had begun to bombard the New City of Jerusalem, Israel military authorities forbade their troops to retaliate with either artillery or air strikes against the Old City. No one will ever number the additional casualties among Israel's finest young men who fell in ferocious hand-to-hand fighting that the City of Peace might not be violated.

A word is in order here about the so-called Arab section of Jerusalem. There never was such a section. For centuries the old walled part of the city—also referred to as East Jerusalem—was inhabited simultaneously by Christians, Moslems, and Jews, each in their own area. Jerusalem was never occupied exclusively by Arabs, was never the capital of an Arab government. For nineteen years—from 1948 to 1967—it was occupied by Jordanian troops because they happened to be there when the armistice lines were drawn ending the War of Liberation which was thrust upon Israel at the very moment of its birth. In our next chapter we shall see how the Jordanians acquitted themselves during their few years of sovereignty over the Holy City. The point to be made here is that Jerusalem was no less "occupied" then than it is now.

One of the most dramatic stories to issue from the

1967 war is that of a military commander who made his troops vow they would reunite Jerusalem no matter how extravagant their losses. They vowed. Then one of the soldiers turned to him and said, "Now *you* vow that once we have won the city with our blood, you and our leaders will never surrender it again!"

Only against this background can we understand the extraordinary behavior of Israeli soldiers when Jerusalem was liberated and the Western Wall, only remnant of the ancient Temple, came again into Jewish hands. Tough, unemotional, battle-hardened veterans stood before the wall and wept unashamedly. Men who had not entered a synagogue or uttered a prayer in years insisted on participating in a religious service. So great was the demand for prayer books and *tefileen* that the supplies of both were quickly exhausted—impressive evidence of the fact that nationalism and religion have always been inextricably interwoven in Judaism.

For Jews, there is a mystique surrounding Jerusalem and the Western Wall, the *Kotel ha-ma-a-ravee*. No one has expressed this with more poetic eloquence than the distinguished teacher of rabbis, Dr. Abraham Joshua Heschel:

The Wall . . . At first I am stunned. Then I see: a Wall of frozen tears, a cloud of sighs. . . .

So tough, so strong, so tenacious. How she survived the contempt of ages! For centuries while garbage was heaped in her front to cover her face, she remained impervious to desecration, mighty, of mysterious majesty in the midst of scorn.

So many different rulers held sway over the city, so many cataclysmic changes, so many upheavals, so many eruptions of passion came to pass—the Wall kept a silent watch. . . .

When Jerusalem was destroyed, we were driven out and like sheep have gone astray; we have turned every one to his own way. The Wall alone stayed on.

What is the Wall? The unceasing marvel. Expectation. The Wall will not perish. The redeemer will come. Silence. I hug the stones; I pray. O, Rock of Israel, make our faith strong and Your words luminous in our hearts and minds. No image. Pour holiness into our moments. . . .

Once you have lived a moment at the Wall, you never go away.

How can I depart from you? You have become a part of me. My bones will forever be filled with your secret.[4]

I can attest personally to this mystique. I am not a mystic. My basic orientation to religion and life is rationalistic, some of my friends would say rigidly so. Yet on each of my visits to Jerusalem since 1967, as I have approached the Wall for the first time, the most intense emotions have suffused my heart, binding me inexplicably to every Jew and every sacred moment of Jewish history since Solomon. Without embarrassment or shame or need to explain intellectually, I have kissed the cold stones of the Wall, kissed them not only for myself but also for my father and grandfather who first imbued me with love for this sacred relic but were never privileged to see it.

It is heartening to report that a few Christian theologians have begun to understand the dynamic of Jerusalem in Jewish thought. Several weeks after the Six Day War, sixteen distinguished professors on the faculties of major Protestant seminaries in the United States issued a public statement which included this paragraph:

Judaism has at its center an indissoluble bond between the people of Israel and the land of Israel. For Christians, to acknowledge the necessity of Judaism is to acknowledge that Judaism presupposes inextricable ties with the land of Israel and the City of David, without which Judaism cannot be truly itself. Theologically, it is this dimension to the religion of Judaism which leads us to support the reunification of the City of Jerusalem.

Several months later two eminent American Catholic theologians spoke in similar vein. Most Christian religious leaders and church bodies have been slow to follow. Over and above the failure to define or understand Judaism with accuracy, Christian theology is involved, too, in their attitude toward Israel.

One factor has been the vast Christian missionary enterprise aimed at the Arab world. Many denominations sponsor hospitals, schools, universities, and colleges on an extensive scale in the Near East in the belief that the Arab world offers a fertile field for conversion. The dubious motives which impel some church leaders to extreme caution in order not to offend the Arabs are not unlike those which fomented anti-Semitism among the earliest Christians in the Roman world when the overwhelming majority of Jews refused to convert to the nascent Christian faith.

Also operating here is the theological notion we have already encountered, that because the Jews rejected Jesus as the messiah, they are doomed by divine destiny to be an accursed, wandering people. Their return to the ancient homeland before they have accepted Christianity is thus an affront to God Himself.

Emil Fackenheim has expressed the Jewish view:

> Why should Christian spokesmen have remained neutral as between Israel's claim to the right to live and Arab claims to the right to destroy her—if not because of old, unconscious, theologically inspired doubts as to whether the 'fossil' Israel did indeed have the right to live? Why has there always been much Christian concern for Arab refugees from Israel, but none whatever for Jewish refugees from Arab countries—if not because of old, no longer consciously remembered ecclesiastical doctrines to the effect that Jews (unlike Arabs) must be kept landless, and therefore rightless?[5]

Our understanding of the Christian theological approach

to Israel remains incomplete if we fail to note a strange paradox. While one current of Christian thought has asserted that the Jews cannot collectively return to their homeland until after they have accepted Jesus as the Christ, there have been other Christians who held that Christ's second coming cannot occur until after the Jewish people has been reconstituted on its ancient soil. Because of such inconsistent positions on this point, the attitude of Christian theologians, ambivalent at best, has more often been antagonistic than favorable toward the modern state of Israel.

In addition to these theological considerations, a psychological factor of great importance also helps us understand the negative attitude of some Christians to Israel. For many centuries Jews everywhere have constituted a weak and nearly helpless minority. Disdained, condemned, oppressed, without political control or power, we have been more the objects than the subjects of history. Our fate has been largely determined by others, not by ourselves. The devastation wrought against us by Hitler reinforced the image of a weak and powerless people. It also evoked much pity and compassion on our behalf from the Christian world.

But psychologically there is a vast difference between pity and respect. Even some persons who developed genuine compassion for us Jews so long as we remained the minority victims of successive majorities find it difficult to empathize with us when we assume some control over our own destiny. Unconsciously some Christians who are prepared to pity Jewish underlings cannot comfortably accept the idea of Jews as equals. The brief but impressive history of Israel has done much to change the image of the Jew from that of patient petitioner, waiting nervously for others to set the boundaries of his future, to that of one who takes positive action on his own toward determining his fate. An undetermined but significant amount of animosity against Israel, based undeniably on ancient theological prejudice, has been reinforced by this psychological reality.

As a result, certain Christian religious leaders have conspired with Arab political leaders to oppose Zionism. It is a perversion of truth to assert that Zionism is entirely a modern movement, only a version of the nationalistic fervor which pervaded so much of Europe in the latter nineteenth century. It is in part that, of course, but the roots of Zionism go deeper and farther. Nor is it accurate to assume that Zionism is entirely a political, secular movement. Actually, it is the current, organized embodiment of the age-old, religiously motivated yearning of Jews to re-establish a commonwealth in their ancient land. Even Zionist parties and sects which are generally considered to be secular are in fact responding also to the religious imperatives of Jewish tradition.

While anti-Zionism and anti-Semitism are not to be equated, it would be naïve to deny that the former has often served as a quasi-legitimate cloak for the latter. It is not fashionable to be an overt anti-Semite these days, especially not in an avowed democracy like the United States. Both the inner compulsions of the American heritage and the lurid example of the Nazis have made any open expression of anti-Jewish prejudice reprehensible. No one supposes, however, that all such sentiment has suddenly vanished. It appears now in a new guise: Jews are all right; only their involvement with Zionism is objectionable. One of the largest sources of vile anti-Semitism in the United States today is the anti-Israel, anti-Zionist (hence anti-Jewish) propaganda which is distributed, both orally and in print, on the campuses of our universities by Arab exchange students, many of them on full scholarships provided by the United States Government. The infamous nineteenth-century forgery, *The Protocols of the Learned Elders of*

Zion, a major source of anti-Semitic prejudice both in Europe and this country, is still being reprinted and distributed prolifically by the Arabs.

We have seen, then, that both Zionism and anti-Zionism are rooted in theology—the first in Judaism, the second, more often than it should be, in Christianity. Israel has additional meanings, too, for contemporary American Jews, meanings which in any other religious tradition would be considered extra-theological. In Judaism, though they exceed theology in a narrow construction, they cannot be divorced from our deepest religious affirmations.

In a most elementary sense, Israel represents for Jews today the only chance to save the remnant of our decimated, nearly exterminated people. It has been estimated that in the event, God forbid, of a nuclear war, as many as a third or more of the American people might be killed. That would mean roughly 70,000,000, men, women, and children. We Jews do not have to imagine such a catastrophe; through human fiendishness rather than nuclear power, it has already happened to us. Of 16,000,000 Jews in the world when Hitler assumed power, 6,000,000 had lost their lives by 1945. We cannot bring back to life those who have already been transformed into ashes or soap. But we can and must do everything possible to rescue and rehabilitate those who remain. The only place on earth where this can be done—where they can be saved as individuals and as Jews—is Israel. More impressive even than the astounding physical progress of that infant state is the remarkable amalgam of its population of Jewish refugees from all corners of the world. Since the inception of the state in 1948, more than two million of them have been brought there. There are Jews in Israel from more than eighty national and cultural origins, some from the most advanced and sophisticated lands of our century, others who had been living in pre-medieval squalor before their rescue. In Israel

there are Jews whose skins are white, brown, yellow, black
—all with new self-esteem and new reasons for wanting to
live.

An incident which occurred immediately following the
Arab-Israel war of 1973 dramatically illustrates both the
tragedy of twentieth-century Jewry and the inestimable
role of Israel. A friend of mine met an Israeli inquiring
for his missing son on the Golan Heights where the young
man had participated in some of the most ferocious tank
battles of all time against the Syrians. After days of weary
and desperate searching, he finally found his son's watch
in the rubble of an artillery position. It was quite obvious
that the boy had been blown to pieces in the explosion of
his tank.

When the probable truth became inescapable, the old
man broke down. Tearfully he recounted how his entire
family had been lost in the Holocaust; only he and this
young son had escaped. Now he, the aged father, was
literally the only one left—left without a living relative,
without even a grave to visit in the whole world, without a
place to recite *kaddish* over the remains of a wife or child.
That man, and countless others like him, are charges on
the conscience of every responsible Jew—and Christian—in
the world. Only through Israel can we hope to fulfill our
heavy obligation to them.

On a visit to Israel in December of 1964 my wife and
I boarded an immigrant ship shortly after it had reached
the port of Haifa. A Turkish vessel, it had carried a cargo
of human refuse, castoffs from Eastern Europe and North
Africa. Through an interpreter, we spoke with several men
and women from both groups. We learned that those who
had come from behind the Iron Curtain had applied for
exit visas from two to fourteen years before their departure.
The instant they had requested permission to leave, they

had been stripped of citizenship in their native land and had endured an agonizing period of waiting as outcasts, despite the fact that the cost of the visa, which had to be met at once, was so exorbitant it had to be paid for them by the United Jewish Appeal.

If they had occupied positions of status in the national economy, they were immediately deprived of these and compelled to subsist on whatever miserable crumbs of employment they could scavenge. If they had owned apartments, they had to sell them for a pittance, in many cases forced first to redecorate them at their own expense for the new Gentile occupants. They were not permitted to take with them any gold, not even watches or rings. During all the anxious years of waiting, they did not dare conceive a child. For if the number of individuals listed on the original application changed by virtue either of birth or death, the whole process had to be initiated again.

We conversed with one old man from Rumania—about seventy years of age, though it was difficult to judge after what he had endured—who had once owned extensive timberlands. When the lumber industry was nationalized, his property was expropriated without compensation. For a short time the government employed him as a manager on what had been his own land, but soon that too was terminated. His two children had been incinerated at Auschwitz; his eyes bore an unutterable pain. Our interpreter touched the old man's shoulder gently, pointed toward the glistening lights ascending the hill from the port to the summit of Mt. Carmel and asked, "What do you see?" Softly, so softly through his tears that we could scarcely hear, he replied, "It's beautiful—beautiful. Now at last I'm home!"

For all the tragedy that had scarred his life, that man was among the more fortunate. Hosts of others who have suffered as much have not yet succeeded in reaching Israel.

Only a tiny fraction of the three million of them in Russia are permitted to leave. Large numbers in Latin America live precariously from whim to whim of the ruling powers. Israel is the sole, indispensable hope of those who need it.

It is more even than that. We have already spoken of the unique contribution Judaism has made and can continue making to civilization. Israel is the most hopeful setting in the world for the shaping of that contribution. It is the most favorable domicile for the creative Jewish spirit. In order for our collective potential to be realized, there must be one country where Jews are a majority of the population, where our cultural-spiritual environment will prevail. Here in the United States, Judaism will be for us Jews at best a secondary or supplementary civilization. This is as it should be; our primary milieu is American. At best, we shall still be able to keep Judaism alive here, to make it function in our lives and transmit it in relevant terms to our children. We alone shall not succeed in keeping it creative and productive, however, in encouraging it to sprout new values and to mold a new society according to those values. For that, we need Israel.

Israel is where the adventure of Judaism began. Israel is where our covenant with God originated. Even during our people's longest, loneliest nights, when the spirit of Judaism was banished into anguished exile, Israel was the vicarious homeland which our fathers carried in their hearts and which, in turn, sustained their hopes. It is the fertile soil out of which tomorrow's Judaism is most likely to grow.

For the American Jew, there is no conflict between his loyalty to Israel and to the United States, no more than between his love for mother and father. As an American, he feels no civic, political, or military loyalty to Israel. Yet he cannot stand in the Judean Hills without experiencing an intense, mystic bond uniting him to the Psalmist who may have stood on that very spot while singing his songs of praise to God. He cannot spend an hour in the little town of Yavneh without feeling that he belongs with Rabbi Jochanan ben Zakkai, who founded his Academy there. It is impossible for him to pass through Caesarea without associating himself with Rabbi Akiba, who suffered martyrdom there under the heavy hand of Rome.

The American Jew is doubly fortunate. So many of the high ideals emanating from his people's ancient land and motivating its current revival have become the values of America too. He shares a double patrimony. The stronger his devotion to Israel, the richer becomes his dedication to the very best in America. During World War I, long before Israel had been established as a state, United States Supreme Court Associate Justice Louis D. Brandeis voiced this truth with exceptional eloquence: "Let no Americans imagine that Zionism is inconsistent with patriotism. Multiple loyalties are objectionable only if they are inconsistent. A man is a better citizen of the United States for being also a loyal citizen of his state, and of his city; for being loyal to his family, and to his profession or trade; for being loyal to his college or lodge. . . . Every American Jew who aids in advancing the Jewish settlement in Palestine, though he feels that neither he nor his descendants will ever live there, will likewise be a better man, a better American for doing so."[6]

A two-way traffic has developed between the Jewish communities of the United States and Israel. Many Israelis —most of them graduate students and research specialists —come here for periods of study. A few remain permanently; the majority return to utilize their new skills at home. A steady flow of American Jewish visitors travels each year to Israel. A very small number remain; nearly all return, enriched and ennobled by the experience. The

Jew from any other country who visits Israel is not just a tourist; in a very real sense, he is a participant in one of the most exciting and significant human experiments on earth. This was seen and felt almost a generation ago, in 1941, when Dr. Norman MacLean, one-time chaplain to King George VI and former moderator of the General Assembly, Church of Scotland, said: "There is no experiment in human uplift now to be seen on the face of the earth which can compare to the work of the Jews in Palestine [now Israel]. If I were a Jew, I would deem it the highest honor life can hold to take part in a work so noble." The passage of thirty-seven years since these words were spoken has made them even truer than they were originally.

The quality and intensity of Jewish life in the United States have already been appreciably affected by Israel. There has been, for example, a revival of the Hebrew language here. Beyond the liturgical value of Hebrew, to which we have already alluded, conversational and literary Hebrew forms a firm bridge between the two most important Jewish communities of the day. Much Jewish music, literature, intellectual research, and art have come from Israel to enhance our lives here.

The contributions are not limited, however, to one direction. Over and above our sorely needed financial support, there is much that we American Jews can give to Israel. This is true especially in the religious domain. We have seen that the fabric of historic Judaism was woven of two inseparable threads, religion and nationalism. There is a double danger in contemporary Jewish life: we in America may emphasize religion at the expense of ethnic and nationalistic elements; and the Israelis may concentrate on nationalism to the neglect of religion. Either would be a distortion of what Judaism has been and should continue to be. We need each other to restore the proper balance.

Religious life in Israel today poses a strange paradox. Judged by institutional standards, most Jews in Israel do not appear to be religious. They do not affiliate with congregations and, except perhaps for the High Holy Days, do not attend religious services. Some of these are even scornful of organized religion. Yet in other ways they exemplify the best in religion. We have already noted with approval that the average Israeli child has more knowledge of Jewish sources and history than even the better educated Jewish adult in the United States. It is difficult to brand the idealism of the *kibbutzim*, in sacrificing personal interest to the interests of the group, as anything but religious. The spiritual response of so many Israelis to repossession of the western Wall was a religious phenomenon of the highest order.

On his return from a prolonged visit to Israel, Rabbi W. Gunther Plaut of Toronto expressed himself eloquently on this point:

I measure religion by the service of heart and hand and by concern for humanity. On these matters Israel rates very high indeed. For the people of Israel have a sense of mission about them. They desire to be not just another people, but a people with a special moral stature. They feel that they have inherited the living Bible. The Bible is the major textbook in the schools, and the people live in its land where every stone, every tree, every valley and every river speaks with biblical accents. Children know the Bible better than many a rabbi outside of Israel. They know much of it by heart, and their language is interlaced with its phrases. They may be in most regards secular, but the God of the Bible and the moral force of the Bible are on their tongues and in their hearts and in their minds.

Sometimes I feel that when they seem to pay the least heed to the God of Israel, they are in fact doing His work. For when they take in the refugees, when they take in the halt and lame and blind whom nobody else in the world will take, they are religious in the finest sense of the word. When young men and women go out into the desert, to build outposts in the wilderness where water is miles away and the enemy is close at hand; when they go there with no other purpose than to serve their people, they practice religion. When kibbutzniks continue to subscribe to a philosophy of service and voluntarily refuse to chase after wealth or after success as the norm of life, they do the work of God. There is more religion amongst these people than amongst many others who piously go to synagogue regularly and sing the prayers most loudly.[7]

Further indirect evidence of deep religious sentiment, which many Israelis do not even suspect in themselves, is their passion for archaeology. Israel today can almost be described as a nation of archaeologists; thousands upon thousands of its citizens either dig as amateurs in their own environs or follow avidly the latest discoveries of professionals. No sooner had the Western Wall come again into Jewish possession than digging was resumed to learn more about the Temple of King Solomon and the religious regimen which prevailed there almost 3,000 years ago. In part, to be sure, this profound interest in uncovering the past reflects a nationalistic need to fill lacunae in the historic record, but it is more than that. The Bible itself has become a guidebook for archaeology; the people grow almost ecstatic when a place or an event described in the Bible is verified. Every new discovery underscores the immense importance of religion in their collective past. It would be foolish to deny that at least an oblique feeling for religion helps motivate this compulsion to dig, or that such vivid reminders of religion will have significant effect.

The paradox of much genuine inner religious sentiment combined with outer indifference, even antagonism, can be partially understood in terms of Israel's current political situation. With a plethora of political parties, no one of which is able to capture a majority of the electorate, it has been necessary to form a coalition of parties to govern.

Because of Arab enmity and the indifference of so many other nations, the overarching consideration has had to be security. This makes compromise imperative, compromise which is often distasteful to the majority but which must be temporarily accepted if disastrous internal strife is to be averted.

One such set of compromises inheres in the need of Israel's dominant political parties to co-opt the support of the smaller religious parties. British mandatory law had taken over from previous Turkish adminstrations of the land the practice of permitting each faith community to exercise complete power over the religious life of its communicants. Because the only kind of rabbi in Palestine then was the Orthodox rabbi, he automatically assumed this authority for Jews. Thus all matters involving religious or domestic law are handled for Jews by an Orthodox-dominated Ministry of Religious Affairs. Until recently, the only spiritual alternatives for the average Israeli have been Orthodox religion or none. Faced with this choice, at least in a nominal sense most have chosen none.

In the Diaspora—that is to say, among Jewish communities outside Israel—Orthodox Judaism is not monolithic. It includes some who are intransigent and rigid, others who strive—without abandoning the discipline of traditional mores and laws—to reinterpret tradition in the light of modern circumstances. In Israel unfortunately the unyielding variety of Orthodoxy prevails, especially among those who possess political power far beyond their proportion of the population.

This poses a nagging problem for the Israelis. They face the inescapable challenge of shaping a state which will be responsive to the highest values of Jewish religious tradition while at the same time avoiding the pitfalls of theocracy, of corrupting collusion between religious and political power.

Today there are a few struggling Conservative and Reform congregations in Israel. Among the intellectuals as well as the spiritually sensitive youth there is much painful searching for alternatives beyond the two that have so far been available, Orthodoxy and complete secularism. There is good reason to expect that, as the country achieves greater security on the international scene and increased maturity within itself, the search for a variety of Jewishly authentic spiritual orientations will succeed.

Until early 1978 a claim might have been made that such hopes constituted nothing more than wishful thinking. They are now hard reality. In mid-1977 Reform Judaism established ARZA, the Association of Reform Zionists of America, as an affiliate of the Union of American Hebrew Congregations. Simultaneously the Reform Jews of Canada organized a similar group called KADIMAH. In subsequent elections for the World Zionist Congress of February 1978 ARZA, still an infant organization, achieved a success spectacular enough to become a faction of major significance at the Congress itself.

At the Congress sessions in Jerusalem, the ARZA delegation discovered a tremendous restlessness among the Israelis on the issue of religious freedom for non-Orthodox Judaism. They had been waiting for a catalyst and we were able to meet their need. Against the stubborn opposition of Orthodoxy, and with the cooperation of Conservative Jewish leaders, we prompted the Zionist leaders of the world to pass a strong resolution favoring Jewish religious pluralism. The Congress urged Israel "to implement fully the principle of guaranteed religious rights for all its citizens, including equality of opportunity, equality of recognition, and equality of governmental aid to all religious movements within Judaism."

Though only a beginning, this is a hopeful start in the struggle which will end in Israel's acceptance of the same religious choices already enjoyed by Jews in other lands and by Christians and Moslems in Israel.

The ultimate solution will be neither Conservative nor Reform Judaism as they exist in the United States. The Israelis themselves will have to work out their own non-Orthodox variants, in response to their own problems and needs. This has been the pattern of our religious life in the past; it will continue to be in the future. What is required in the meantime, from both Jews and non-Jews outside Israel, is understanding and patience.

CHAPTER TWELVE

A Covenant to the People

> I am the Lord, I have called you in righteousness,
> I have taken you by the hand and kept you;
> I have given you as a covenant to the people,
> For a light to the nations,
> To open the eyes that are blind,
> To bring out the prisoners from the dungeon,
> From the prison those who sit in darkness. . . .

Thus did Isaiah, twenty-six centuries ago, describe the role of ancient Israel among the nations. The potential of modern Israel is as challenging. It can mean as much to the world as to its own inhabitants and their Jewish brothers. There should be no need to expand on the immense importance of the first two Jewish commonwealths to Christianity. From the first came the foundations of Judaism, and most especially the Hebrew Bible, with its messianic expectations so indispensable to the Christian faith. From the second came Jesus and Paul and the new faith. Without ancient Israel, there could have been no Judaism. Without ancient Israel, therefore, there would have been no Christianity. What opportunity, what promise, does modern Israel hold for Christians?

On the lowest level of self-interest, the safety and survival of Christian communities throughout the Middle East will be enhanced by a secure Israel. A case in point is the blatant persecution of the Coptic Christians over a long period of time by Egypt. More recent and dramatic are the violent attempts by Arab Moslem factions in Lebanon to destroy the influence if not even the physical presence of Christians, among them Arab Christians. From the end of World War I into the mid-1970s the destiny of Lebanon hinged on a very delicate, precarious balance in governmental control between its Christian and Moslem populations. That balance has subsequently been upset as Arafat's battalions have mounted strong military pressure against the Christians. It is no exaggeration to say that had it not been for strong support from Israel, the Christian communities of southern Lebanon might well have been exterminated. This makes all the more paradoxical and ironic the indifference, even antagonism, which so many Christian churches and spokesmen have shown toward the fate of Israel. But the modern Jewish State offers higher dimensions of meaning to Christians than just their own security.

Among them, a chance to execute justice. Justice here is no simple or easy objective. There are Arabs as well as Jews in Israel and the Middle East; they too demand and deserve justice. Is there any way to adjudicate the competitive claims of two peoples? Surely the initial requirement must be to seek truth, to know the facts accurately.

Justice requires us to recognize that since the end of World War I the Arabs in the Middle East have achieved twenty-two independent nations, encompassing some five and a half million square miles. By international mandate the Jews have attained their only independent nation— Israel—in a territory measuring eight thousand square miles. The area of undisputed Jewish sovereignty in comparison with Arab-ruled states is as that of New Jersey to six times that of Texas.

Justice necessitates also that we ask how the anguish of

the Arab refugees originated. The answer is astonishingly simple. There were no Arab refugees prior to 1948. Their appearance was precipitated by the unjust attack against Israel launched by all seven surrounding Arab governments at the very instant of the new state's birth. On May 14, 1948—the very day the Israelis proclaimed their national independence—Abdul Rahman Pasha Azzam, Secretary-General of the Arab League, was quoted on a British Broadcasting Corporation newscast as saying: "This will be a war of extermination and a momentous massacre which will be spoken of like the Mongolian massacres and the Crusades." He did not exaggerate Arab intentions.

Even after it had been brutally assaulted, Israel strove valiantly but vainly to persuade its Arab population not to flee. The British, loosing their mandatory ties to the area and anything but friendly to Jewish aspirations and hopes, issued an official police report in Haifa on April 26, 1948: "Every effort is being made by the Jews to persuade the Arab populace to stay and carry on with their normal lives, to get their shops and businesses open and to be assured that their lives and interests will be safe."[1]

Meanwhile, an appeal was distributed to the Arabs of Haifa on April 28, 1948, by the Haifa Workers' Council. In both Hebrew and Arabic it said: "Do not fear! Do not destroy your homes with your own hands; do not block off your sources of livelihood; and do not bring upon yourself tragedy by unnecessary evacuation and self-imposed burdens. By moving out you will be overtaken by poverty and humiliation. But in this city, yours and ours, Haifa, the gates are open for work, for life, and for peace, for you and your families."

Why did so many Arabs flee despite such fervent pleas? First, because—knowing what they would do to the Jews had the situation been reversed—the Arabs feared the worst. Second, because their own leaders urged them to vacate in order to make room for the invading Arab armies, promising that they would soon be able to return and to expropriate much booty from the murdered Jews. This was clearly recognized by authoritative sources at the time. The *London Economist* of October 2, 1948, reported the following concerning Haifa's Arab population: "Various factors influenced their decision to seek safety in flight. There is but little doubt that the most potent of these were the announcements made over the air by the Arab Higher Executive, urging all Arabs in Haifa to quit. The reason given was that upon the final withdrawal of the British the combined armies of the Arab States would invade Palestine and drive the Jews into the sea, and it was clearly intimated that those Arabs who remained in Haifa and accepted Jewish protection would be regarded as renegades."

In moments of self-disclosure which they probably later regretted, some of the Arab leaders themselves revealed the truth. On September 6, 1948, the Secretary of the Palestine Arab Higher Committee, Emile Ghoury, said, "The fact that there are these refugees is the direct consequence of the act of the Arab States in opposing partition and the Jewish State. The Arab States agreed upon this policy unanimously, and they must share in the solution of the problem."

The Arab refugees are usually thought of as having been forced from their homes into conditions of destitute displacement. Not all of them by any means fit this description. *The Survey of International Affairs* has confirmed the fact that as early as January 1948—four months before Israel declared its independence and was invaded by Arab armies —there was a "steady exodus" of middle-class Arab families, carrying with them considerable quantities of property and wealth. Much publicity has been given to the Arabs living in the squalor and misery of camps; the world has paid scant attention to the fact that there are also Arab "refugees" in Amman, capital of Jordan, whose homes are luxurious.

The truth, then, is self-evident. The refugee problem was created by the Arabs themselves: first, by attacking Israel, second, by urging their kinsmen to flee. Expansion of the refugee problem after the Six Day War of 1967 occurred in part for the same reason. Those Arabs who fled from the west bank of the Jordan River during the hostilities did so at their own initiative. They were not forced to flee. Those who fled because of honest, even if misguided, fear and had no nefarious designs against Israel were allowed to return. Large numbers of refugees from 1948 were in camps located in the Gaza Strip and on the west bank, territories occupied by Israel since June 1967. If they wished to depart for Egypt or Jordan, they were permitted to do so. If they remained, they have already received more humane treatment from Israel than they had known for nearly two decades at the hand of their own flesh. One of the most amazing aspects of the 1967 conflict was the loyalty of the quarter-million Arabs who were then citizens of Israel. There was not the slightest movement on their part to aid the other Arabs in their renewed attempt to destroy the state.

How many bona fide refugees were there in 1948? The answer depends upon whom we ask and when. The original U.N. estimate was 600,000 to 650,000. Ten years later the figure most commonly used ranged from 900,000 to 1,000,000. By 1966 there was talk of a million and a quarter and more recently Arab propagandists have irresponsibly and inaccurately inflated the total to as many as 3,000,000. Why the discrepancies? For one thing, every birth was faithfully recorded and a new ration card issued. Almost no deaths were reported; an astonishingly large number of dead Arabs are still officially listed as living refugees. Some indigenous Arabs in Jordan and Egypt, moreover, attached themselves voluntarily to the refugee camps because, as miserable as standards were there, they were significantly superior to conditions in the Arab states. In 1959 two United States Senators, conducting an investigation of the refugee relief program for the Senate Committee on Foreign Relations, reported that the government of Jordan was then refusing to invalidate refugee ration cards which should have expired eleven years before. In one sample group examined by these senators, 42 per cent of the operative cards were proven to be fraudulent!

A simple exercise in elementary arithmetic can help clarify the probable number of legitimate Arab refugees. In 1922 there were 184,000 Arabs residing in the area which later became Israel. By 1947—attracted by the economic, cultural, and medical improvements resulting from Jewish settlement—their numbers had increased from 184,000 to 750,000. British census figures from 1921 to 1944 indicate that in areas of substantial Jewish settlement the Arab population increased sevenfold; elsewhere in Palestine that increase was 50 per cent. This means—plainly and incontrovertibly—that when Israel came into being three Arabs of every four residing within its borders had been there less than a generation. It must be remembered also that in 1949 more than a quarter of a million Arabs lived, by their own choice, within Israel as citizens. In the light of these realities, to speak of more than a million Arab refugees from Israel must be attributed either to mathematical ignorance or malicious distortion.

Yet the refugees are there and their needs cry out to every decent human being. Whatever the numbers, their plight is pitiful. It must weigh heavily on the conscience of all. What has been done to help them?

By the Arabs themselves, nothing. The very Arab governments which had originally encouraged the refugees to leave home have callously refused either to aid them or to integrate them into their own societies. They prefer to keep them as pawns, as potential weapons against Israel. Many of them have been trained to invade Israel as guerrilla terrorists. Whatever aid the camps have received has come through the United Nations, principally from the United States. Israel has contributed more to United Nations relief for Arab refugees than any of the Arab nations, even the wealthiest.

In 1957 the Research Group for European Migration Problems concluded: " . . . The Arab Governments have been applying to the refugees an abstract and inhuman policy: for the purpose of maintaining a menacing population on the frontier with Israel, these Governments have systematically rejected all organization and employment for the refugees. . . . *Their attitude is one of seeking to prevent any sort of adaptation and integration, because the refugees are seen as a political means of pressure to get the greatest number of concessions.*" [Italics added.] The contrast is all the more stark if we recall that this obdurate insensitivity obtained precisely during the years when more than a half-million hapless Jewish refugees from Arab lands were being warmly welcomed by Israel and integrated into its social structure.

What has Israel attempted to do for the Arab refugees? Here we come upon a compelling paradox. Israel, so often and so unjustly accused of indifference to the plight of the Arabs, has in fact demonstrated far more concern for them than have their own Arab kinsmen. Almost immediately after the war which had been intended to demolish the new state—in August of 1949—Israel offered to readmit 100,000 refugees. The Arabs refused to accept the offer, lest by so doing they would imply recognition of Israel's existence! Despite this rebuff, Israel allowed 50,000 Arabs to return so that their divided families could be reunited.

Between $10,000,000 and $11,000,000 in frozen assets— chiefly bank accounts abandoned by fleeing Arabs—were released by Israel, even though this meant sending desperately needed hard currency into the very countries which are attempting to strangle the Jewish state by boycott. Israel has repeatedly announced its readiness to compensate the refugees for their property as part of a general peace settlement. The Arab nations have stubbornly refused to have any part of such a settlement. Time and again, with persistence and patience, Israel has pleaded with the Arabs to sit down together for peace talks. Their offers have been rejected; the Arab governments want no peace, they want only the annihilation of Israel and its population. Except for Egypt, they refuse even to sit down in the same room with Israelis for discussions; all such contacts have been by third-party intermediaries shuttling back and forth between delegations representing respectively the Israelis and Arabs. The latter, moreover, have insisted that a precondition for any general peace conference—not a matter to be determined through *bona fide* negotiation but a *precondition*—be the total withdrawal of Israel from all lands administered by it as a result of the 1967 war. Israel has offered to negotiate return of some of this territory, provided this be part of a permanent border adjustment and peace. The Arab response has been only a sullen, truculent threat to destroy Israel "next time."

One of Israel's first actions after the victory of 1967 was to announce its willingness to permit some of the new refugees to return at once from Jordan to their former homes on the west bank. Despite weeks of negotiation, very few of them came back. The government of Jordan refused to accept as valid entry forms officially stamped by Israel as well as by the Red Cross. Seven thousand permits authorizing the return of former Arab residents to the occupied west bank remained unused. These were extended for another three months in early 1969; when the extension period ended, 6,000 permits had still not been claimed.

Apparently the Arab refugees or the government of Jordan would prefer to perpetuate their complaint rather than accord even implicit recognition to the legitimacy of Israel. Contrast this with the post-victory pronouncement of Elieser Livneh, one of Israel's leading journalists: "We are Jews and the State is Jewish; this obligates us even more in the hour of victory. Our first obligation is compensation and reparations to the refugees who lost property in Israel and a large fund to rehabilitate them." These words acquire added significance in view of the government's announcement that it was prepared to contribute £1,000,000 (almost $300,000) to the U.N. agency which provides help for the Arab refugees.

Many people are under the impression that the key to peace in the Middle East is the refugee problem, that if Israel would only deal with it magnanimously, the Arab nations would respond in kind. Nothing could be farther from the truth. We have already seen that Israel's generous gestures in this direction have been spurned and that the Arabs want to extend the suffering of the refugees as a political weapon against Israel.

The real objective of the Arabs is not an equitable resolution of the refugee problem but the extinction of Israel and the extermination of its Jews. In a moment of extraordinary honesty, Nasser made this clear before the Egyptian National Council on March 26, 1964. He said, "Israel imagines that the elimination of the refugee problem will bring about the elimination of the Palestine problem, but it is in the very existence of Israel that the danger is hidden."

The same sentiment was echoed on June 28, 1967, by Iraq's Chief of State, General Abdul Rahman Arif: "The existence of Israel is in itself an aggression and must therefore be repulsed. . . ." In short, nothing will really satisfy or appease the Arab leaders except the demise of Israel.

Since 1967 Arab leaders have spoken with two voices. For foreign consumption, especially here in the United States, they sometimes seem to have become more moderate, pleading for a bi-national state, for the right of Israelis and Arabs to live together peacefully in the same land. When addressing their compatriots at home, however, these leaders still urge the total destruction of Israel.

The "national covenant" adopted by the Palestine Liberation Organization (PLO) in 1964, amended and reaffirmed in 1968, has never been repudiated or modified. Fifteen of the covenant's thirty-three articles call for or imply the elimination of Israel. Article 19, for example, says: "The establishment of Israel is fundamentally null and void." A Palestine National Council meeting in March 1977 refused to make any changes in the covenant. The declaration issued by this Council after eight days of deliberation "called for a continuation of the 'armed struggle' against Israel and rejected recognition of Israel or the signing of any complete peace agreement."[2]

Most Jews see the distinction between Arab extremists and moderates as spurious. A moderate is one who is willing to accomplish tomorrow or the next day what an extremist insists must be done today. Let Israel be forced back first to its vulnerable pre-1967 borders, with Soviet-encouraged Arab armies aiming lethal weapons from all sides, with the width of the country reduced at one point to nine miles. For Arab "moderates," that will suffice for the nonce. After that has been accomplished, it should be relatively easy to destroy the Jewish State while the nations that have "guaranteed" its survival procrastinate and debate. Shades of Chamberlain and Czechoslavakia!

Yasir Arafat, leader of the PLO, and Anwar Sadat, President of Egypt, are frequently cited as Arab "moderates." Let them be judged by their own words:

Arafat in 1977: "I am not a man for settlement or concessions. I will carry on the struggle until every inch of
Palestinian soil will be retrieved . . . ."[3]

Sadat in 1977: "It is not permissible that some should
speak about secure boundaries, which is an obsolete
Israeli concept . . . we will not cede a single inch of
Arab land . . . our national territory is not open to
bargaining."[4]

In November 1977 Sadat startled the world by accepting
Prime Minister Begin's invitation to visit Jerusalem,
where he addressed the Knesset and pleaded for peace.
Subsequently Mr. Begin reciprocated by conferring with
Sadat in Egypt. For a while observers were caught up in
euphoric hope that peace between Israel and its Arab
neighbors was at long last a realistic possibility. The en-
thusiasm of that moment has since been considerably
curbed, however, by the following factors: (1) Sadat has
offered Israel nothing more than recognition of its elementary right to exist, a right to which it is entitled as a
member of the United Nations, and which is not contin-
gent upon the largess of any one leader or power. (2) In
return, the Egyptian President insists that prior to negotiations Israel agree to relinquish every inch of the territory it has held since 1967. This would mean returning
to borders which have been proven to be frightfully inde-
fensible, reducing Israel's girth at one point to nine miles.
UN Resolution 242, which calls upon Israel to withdraw
from occupied lands, does not specify that such withdrawal must be from *all* such lands. The omission was deliberate, reflecting recognition of the fact that total withdrawal would restore the ominous threat which preceded
and precipitated the 1967 war. (3) It was Sadat, not Begin,
who suddenly and inexplicably broke off Egyptian-
Israeli negotiations in January 1978 at a time when considerable progress was being made toward a declaration

of principle which would govern further negotiations. Thus did the Egyptian President signal his determination not to proceed unless assured in advance that *all* his demands would be granted. (4) Sadat speaks only for himself and a segment of the Egyptian people. No other Arab ruler or nation has agreed to recognize Israel even on the impossible terms he proposes. Between 1948 and 1973 there were eighty revolutions in Arab countries—thirty of them successful—and twenty-two leaders have been assassinated. Even if Israel were to accept Sadat's intention at face value, the violence and instability of the Arab world offers little assurance that the concessions demanded would bring Israel the security it needs. (5) Sadat has never renounced the pro-Hitler views he expressed during and since World War II. He was jailed for helping a Nazi spy ring in Egypt to communicate with Field Marshal Rommel's headquarters when the German forces seemed to be on the verge of invading Egypt. Many times since, he has expressed extremely anti-Jewish prejudice. Even after launching his peace initiative, in order to justify rupturing his negotiations with Israel he allowed the fully-controlled Egyptian press which reflects official government opinion to describe Mr. Begin as "Shylock, the Merchant of Venice in Shakespeare's famous story of the Jewish usurer exacting his pound of flesh."

There are differences of opinion among Jews—both in Israel and the United States—on how flexible the government of Israel can afford to be in dealing with peace proposals. There is total agreement, however, that Israel must not compromise its security or survival. In the light of persistent Arab hostility and broken international promises, it will require more than verbal assurances or even treaties to convince the leaders of Israel that they can afford to be as generous as some observers would like them to be.

All genuine seekers of peace must continue to hope

that Sadat will yet restore the mood he created with his dramatic gestures and words of November 1977. If he really means to negotiate, not dictate, if he is honest in desiring peace, not a camouflage for the eventual destruction of the Jewish State, Israel will respond in a manner which can bring blessing to the entire Middle East, indeed the whole world.

The Arabs have consistently claimed that they are not anti-Jewish, only anti-Zionist. In addition to their exploitation of the *Protocols of the Learned Elders of Zion,* already mentioned, the textbooks used in their schools belie this distinction. Dr. Moshe Ma'oz, Professor of Arabic Studies at the Hebrew University in Jerusalem, has done a thorough study of those books. He generally identifies with Arab culture, respecting it and speaking of it with warm praise. His conclusion about the literary material on which a generation of Arab children is being nourished:

> . . . If you read many of the books in Arab countries today, including public school textbooks approved by the respective governments, you find countless passages urging hatred of all Jews, not only Zionists, and exhorting them to kill Jews. This type of conditioning helps explain why the animosities are so deep-seated.[5]

In recent years the Arabs have ceased speaking of refugees, emphasizing instead the rights of the *Palestinians* or the *Palestine nation.* The term *Palestine* is used by them to mean the territories legally assigned to Israel. This is a distortion of fact. *Palestine* always referred to what is now Jordan as well as Israel. It has already been partitioned between Arabs and Jews, to the enormous advantage of the former. Only 20 per cent of the territory originally encompassed by the Balfour Declaration was assigned in 1947 by the United Nations to Israel. What is now proposed is that another Arab state be created, forgetting that most of the Jordanians are Palestinians who already have their own sovereign state.

There are two standards by which the declared intentions of the Israelis toward Arab refugees may be judged. One is their magnanimous record of assistance to the newly emerging nations of Africa. They have sent experts in many fields to train the Africans and have invited large numbers of them to study in Israel. I have followed in amazement a group of blackskinned students as they walked on the campus of the Technion outside Haifa, chatting in Hebrew! The new, young nations were at first willing to accept from Israel economic aid which arouses their suspicion when offered by some of the larger powers; they knew that Israel had no imperial designs.

Though Israel is one of the smallest nations in the world, its foreign aid has already reached seventy countries. In a span of ten years 10,500 persons were brought to Israel for training, while 2,500 Israeli technicians were sent abroad for this purpose. One Moslem country, Iran, has received assistance from Israel in rebuilding an area devastated by earthquake. When President Nasser of Egypt visited Ethiopia in 1963, his plane landed on a runway built by Israelis and he was guarded by Israeli-trained secret policemen. What the Jerusalem government has so generously done for nations many miles removed, it would like even more to do for its closer neighbors.

If this enviable example of international altruism has at least temporarily ended, the fault is not Israel's. Unfortunately—and to their own eventual disadvantage—many of the African nations have been persuaded by Arab and Soviet propaganda and by "petrodollar" pressure that Israel is their enemy rather than potentially their most stalwart friend.

The other test of Israel's attitude toward the refugees is the treatment received by those Arabs who are citizens

of Israel, more than 300,000 of them. Their standards of
living and schooling are incomparably higher than those of
their fellows who live in surrounding countries. They participate fully in every aspect of government, even electing
some of their own number to the national parliament, the
Knesset. They edit and publish their own papers. They
have equal access to a magnificent network of hospitals
and clinics, as a result of which diseases which remain en-
demic among their people across the borders have been
eliminated among them.

Many observers make the mistake of viewing the Jews
of Israel as intruders on an indigenous native population. This is historically untrue. Long after the end of Jewish sovereignty in the first century of the Common Era, a
majority of Palestine's population continued to be Jewish. Jewish occupancy has been uninterrupted from that
time to this. In some areas, such as Peki-in in Galilee,
Jewish families today trace their ancestry to Jews who
lived there in antiquity.

Few Arab residents in or refugees from Israel can claim
such long-term ties. Indeed, we have already observed that
a considerable proportion of them entered the country only
after World War I, enticed by the higher living standards
resulting from Jewish enterprise. A Christian historian,
James Parkes, speaking of the countries in the Middle
East, has written: "Apart from neolithic survivals and the
Copts in Egypt, Jews are the longest settled of the present
identifiable inhabitants in some, and have lived longer in
all the others, than Arabs have in Palestine or Egypt."[6]

In making judgments on the situation in the Middle East
and selecting policies most consistent with their own religious principles, Christians would do well to keep in mind
the words spoken before the U.N. as it discussed the Arab-
Israel war of 1956. Golda Meir, then Israel's Foreign Minister, articulated the spirit and will of her entire nation
when she said in March of 1957:

Can we, from now on—all of us—turn a new leaf, and instead of fighting with each other, can we all, united fight poverty, disease, and illiteracy? Is it possible for us to put all our efforts into one single purpose, the betterment and progress and development of all our lands and all our peoples? I can here pledge the government and people of Israel to do their part in this united effort. There is no limit to what we are prepared to contribute so that all of us, together, may live to see a day of happiness for all humanity.

To those who have followed previous chapters carefully it is already apparent that Christendom bears a heavy burden of guilt for the sorry fate suffered by Jews over a span of sixteen centuries. It is neither accident nor coincidence that the most tragic epochs in Jewish history commenced with the establishment of Christianity as the official faith of the Roman Empire. During the Crusades, the Inquisition, the Czarist pogroms in nineteenth-century Russia, the Church was often a direct instigator of persecution and massacre. Everywhere it fostered a theological climate which made it easier for malevolent men to persecute and destroy Jews. Both Protestant and Catholic authorities recognize this truth and have expressed the earnest hope that their religious bodies may now atone for the past. No atonement could be more appropriate or effective than strong support of Israel.

Catholic recognition of this truth was eloquently expressed during the Six Day War by John Delury, secretary of the San Francisco Archdiocesan Commission on Social Justice:

At this moment of grave crisis Christians cannot view the threat to Israel's existence with detachment. We are morally committed to Israel's survival. We are morally committed because of the centuries of Christian persecution of Jews. . . . We are morally committed because Nazi anti-Semitism, though racist and not religious in immediate origin, capitalized on the Jew-as-scapegoat. . . .

> We are morally committed because of the passivity of
> so many Christians in response to the anti-Semitism
> of very recent times. . . .

> There are complexities in the Middle East situation.
> There must be an answer to the Arab refugee prob-
> lem. . . . But one factor stands out clearly: The survival
> of Israel is not only a Jewish concern; it is a Christian
> concern.[7]

Few Christians have understood and admitted their guilt
for the Holocaust or acknowledged their need to expiate
that guilt by supporting Israel more sympathetically than
a group of about 120 Christians who founded and live in
Nes Ammim ("an ensign for the nations"), a village in
western Galilee. In the late 1950s the Synod of the Dutch
Reformed Church published a booklet that urged, in the
light of what happened to the Jewish people during the
Hitler years, a "theological rethinking" of Christian-Jewish
relations. A series of discussions based on this booklet led
to the founding of *Nes Ammim* in 1962. Its members—now
a few Swiss, German, British, and American Christians
mixed with the original Dutch—are pledged to avoid every
semblance of missionary effort and to help Israel by living
there. Christine Pilon, one of the village's founders, has
expressed their motivation and spirit in these words: "We
knew that what had happened in Germany was not just
the work of one maniac or even of one country. It was the
extreme expression of anti-Semitism that lies within Christianity itself."

Another dimension of meaning which Israel should have
for the Christian world is the opportunity to cherish and
tend those places and buildings which are preciously associated with the life of Jesus and the earliest beginnings
of Christianity. Our common attachment to the spiritually
fertile soil that gave birth to both our faiths should provide
us with indelible bonds of union and affection. Ironically,

it has instead too often led to friction not only between the Jewish world and the Christian, but even among the many branches of the Christian Church. Israel honors and respects the holy places of its two daughter religions no less than its own.

On my first visit to Israel, during Passover of 1958, I recall standing in line on the steps leading to the upper room at the Church of the Dormition in Jerusalem, the chamber in which the Last Supper is believed to have occurred. As we awaited admission to the room, we overheard a conversation between a Jewish father and his son, a boy of perhaps nine or ten years, about the Jewish festival of Passover and the Christian Easter. The father told his little boy in Hebrew the New Testament story of the Last Supper, explaining to him why the room they were about to see was a place of special meaning to Christians. The solemn respect they both showed is typical of the way the Jews of Israel have always treated the sanctities of all the religions which share sacred ties to their land.

In the War of Liberation the penalty for desecration of a structure sacred to any religion was death. At the conclusion of that conflict the Nazareth Town Council, consisting of Arabs—Christian and Moslem—proclaimed that their respective holy places had been treated by the Israelis with utmost respect. A Roman Catholic priest, then in charge of his denomination's properties in Nazareth, added: "I would like to say our relations are excellent. We had a few complaints at the beginning, but within an hour after Israeli occupation the Israeli commander, showing great deference to the religious and holy places, made all arrangements for their protection here." This became a precedent, a pattern that has been consistently followed ever since.

Mention has already been made of the fact that after Jordan had rejected Israel's offer to keep Jerusalem free of combat in 1967, the Jewish fighting forces were given strict orders that East Jerusalem would have to be taken without either artillery or air support, so that no edifice sacred to any faith would be damaged or destroyed. This order reflected enormous respect and self-control, especially in view of the fact that the Jordanians had placed many of their gun batteries precisely in and near the holy places, counting on Israel to keep them inviolate.

Every Christian religious authority who has visited Israel has attested to the continuing solicitude of the government and people for the sacred sites. Typical of their testimony is this observation by the Greek Orthodox Patriarch Benedictus: "Everyone has shown kindness and willingness to serve us and all have shown respect for the holy places, churches, convents, and religious institutions."

A British Gentile reporter, Colin Simpson, was with frontline Israeli troops who took Jerusalem on June 7, 1967. He subsequently wrote: "One of the really impressive things was the tremendous care taken by the Israelis not to damage private or religious property. Every soldier I saw seemed to venerate the city and several times held his fire when sniped on from a church roof."[8]

Two months after the 1967 war had been concluded, Bishop José Concalves da Costa visited Israel in his official capacity as Secretary-General of the National Conference of Brazilian Bishops. On the basis of personal observation he supported the reunification of Jerusalem and confirmed Israel's guarantee of free access to all Christian religious pilgrims who wished to visit the sacred sites of their faith in Jerusalem or anywhere else.[9]

In September of 1968 the Israel government negotiated agreements with fifteen churches and religious orders, providing total payments of $1.5 million for repair of minor damage done to sacred edifices during the Six Day War. The Israelis included in this sum all damage, whether caused by themselves or the armies of Jordan.[10]

The Arab record is in sharp contrast. During the nineteen

years that Jordan occupied East Jerusalem by virtue of military invasion and occupation in 1948, Christian, Moslem and Jewish inhabitants of Israel were not permitted to visit their shrines in the Old City. This ban was in direct violation of the 1949 armistice, which also provided Jews with the right of access to the Hebrew University and Hadassah Hospital on Mt. Scopus; this proviso, too, the Arabs refused to honor. Of thirty-five synagogues and Jewish religious institutions in the ancient part of the city, all but one were destroyed. The Jewish cemetery on the Mount of Olives was bulldozed so that a road could be pushed through to a new hotel; 38,000 of its 50,000 graves were defaced or destroyed. Tombstones were used by the Jordanians to pave a path to their army latrines. The moment Israel reoccupied East Jerusalem, the voices of religious leaders everywhere were raised in concern over care of the holy places. For nearly two decades before that, no one seemed to know or care about the scandalous behavior of the Jordanians.

The record is clear. Any truly religious person, anxious for reverent and loving care of the sites sacred to three great religions, should know beyond doubt under whose auspices that care is most likely to be forthcoming.

We have still not exhausted the potential significance of Israel for the entire world. Humanity does not need new ideals today. The values and goals envisaged by the biblical prophets are quite adequate for our age. The trouble is not with the blueprints, but with the fact that they have never in good conscience been implemented. Perhaps the greatest ultimate contribution of Israel, the land from which these designs emanated, is to demonstrate how they can be put into practice. One area in which this may be accomplished is that of economic justice, a major concern of Moses and the prophets who followed him.

Israel today is a laboratory for experimentation with almost every conceivable kind of economic system. The *kibbutzim*, already described, are based on pure communism in the ownership of property—that is, not political or dictatorial communism, but the belief that each should work for all and all should provide for the needs of each. At the other extreme is large-scale private capitalism much like that in the United States. Between the two are all possible variations. The *moshavim*, agricultural cooperatives in which each family owns its own land, arrange for all purchases and sales to be conducted jointly with maximum benefit to all. The Jewish National Fund fosters ownership and development of natural resources by the entire people. The *Histadrut*, Israel's national labor federation, is far more than such an organization would be in this country; it owns a number of industrial enterprises, including the nation's largest construction firm and bus system. In short, Israel is not frozen to any one economic plan. There is room for experimentation and comparison, out of which perhaps a new combination will emerge which can combine maximum productivity with a greater measure of economic justice than has been achieved by any other society.

Many problems must be solved before any such ideal solution will be possible. The *kibbutz* movement is no longer, as it once was, the prevailing economic unit of the country. Rapid economic development, especially for the purpose of absorbing large numbers of desperate immigrants, and the truly staggering cost of military defense against Arab nations that have vowed to destroy Israel have necessitated an increased investment of private capital and the development of industry. The balance is at times precarious between those whose primary purpose is the achievement of maximum private profit and those who concentrate on creating a just and equitable economy.

Nowhere else on earth, however, is there so broad a spectrum of economic experimentation within the boundaries of a single nation.

Israel may also yet provide humanity with its best remaining hope for the attainment of love and peace. Is it strange to hope for love and peace from a land which has been so lavishly bathed in blood, not only in recent decades but throughout much of history? Yet this land was also the source of our most ennobling visions and dreams, dreams of a time when each of us would love all others as he loves himself, when nations would "beat their swords into plowshares and their spears into pruning-hooks."

Much of what has already been written discloses the remarkable application of Jewish ethics to concrete problems in Israel today. In a strange, almost mystical way this people, which never adopted a doctrine of turning the other cheek in theory, seems to have approached the practice of such an ideal more closely than has any other society. There is ample cause for Israelis to despise the British; during the mandatory regime Great Britain did everything possible to subvert the promise implicit in the Balfour Declaration that she would promote the establishment of a Jewish national homeland in Palestine. Especially during the dreadful days of Hitler, Britain exhibited incredible callousness and cruelty to homeless, persecuted Jews who had no other place of refuge. Yet in Israel now there is not the slightest trace of animosity against the British; to the contrary, much British influence remains evident.

A similar attitude toward the community of nations was displayed after the war of 1956. That conflict ended with Israel's forces occupying the Sinai desert all the way to the Strait of Tiran, which connects the Gulf of Aqaba to the Red Sea. The United Nations asked Israel to withdraw its victorious army in favor of international supervision both there and on the border with Egypt. On numerous previous occasions the U.N. had reacted to Israel's desperate needs with pious tongue and paralyzed hand. It would have been understandable had the Israeli authorities stood fast, refusing to acquiesce in the international clamor for withdrawal, but Israel did pull back its soldiers—almost immediately. This move was more than just a surrender to external pressure; at least in part it was also a response to the message of the original Sinai. Despite previous disappointment and betrayal, Israel chose still to trust the world community, to accede to what seemed to be the righteous policy, even at some risk to its own security.

If Israel has been less tractable since the 1967 conflict, if its attitude toward the U.N. has to some extent soured, let it be remembered that the worst fears of 1956 were substantiated. The internationally promised support proved to be illusory; eleven years later the Strait of Tiran was again illegally occupied by Egypt; the U.N. truce force was evacuated at Nasser's demand, and Israel's security, achieved in 1956 at appalling cost of human life, had vanished. So far as its approach to Israel is concerned, the U.N. has shown itself to be an agency of cynical conspiracy rather than of equity or justice. Remnants of age-old anti-Semitism, blended with the imperialist urgencies of the Soviet Union and the Arab nations, have time and again created automatic majorities against Israel. Decisions are rendered not on a basis of issues or merit, but, instead, of naked power. The U.N. has come close to discrediting itself in blackballing Israel from its regional council of UNESCO and branding as racism a Zionist philosophy which is one of the most humane movements of liberation in the world. Yet so urgent is Israel's yearning for peace that it has remained in the U.N., exposing itself continually to unwarranted calumny and libel.

A similar craving for peace explains the remarkable patience of most Israelis and their government toward their Semitic cousins.

One could scarcely blame the Israelis if, after all they have suffered at the hand of Arab truculence and intransigence, a bitter hatred had developed against the Arabs; but this has been avoided too, as evidenced by Israel's treatment of its own Arab citizens and its attitude toward peaceful relations with the Arab nations.

Nowhere was this more dramatically evident than in the behavior of the Israelis during and after the war of 1967. Not one case of rape was reported. Looting was virtually nonexistent. There was no brutality against the enemy. Jewish soldiers shared their precious water in the Sinai desert with their Arab prisoners. They almost seemed embarrassed at the need to wound and kill in self-defense. In the whole of human history there has probably never been a victorious army such as this!

Golda Meir spoke for the entire nation when she movingly addressed these words to the Arabs: "We can forgive you for killing our sons; we can never forgive you for forcing us to kill yours!"

A poignant incident occurred on one of the very few occasions during the 1967 conflict when Israeli troops returned to their base with booty taken from Arabs. Quietly their commanding officer called them together and, without explanation or introduction, began to read them passages from the Bible which prohibited their ancestors from taking booty during military conquest. One by one his men relinquished whatever they had appropriated and the whole of it was returned. One competent observer has summarized the attitude of the victorious Israelis as follows: "The most striking thing about them is their singular lack of hatred for the Arabs, their conviction that they had no choice but to fight, and their almost apologetic feeling about their victory, as though they were somehow at fault for having defended themselves too well."[11]

This restraint followed the pattern established during Israel's War of Liberation, forced upon it by the Arabs in 1948. Even in the heat of battle, there was only one instance of brutal aggression against a civilian Arab village, and those who were responsible for this incident, members of an unauthorized militia called Irgun, were indicted and punished by the authorities in Jerusalem. Later investigation revealed, moreover, that the village in question, Deir Yassin, had harbored Arab troops used to ambush Jewish soldiers trying to rescue the inhabitants of Jerusalem, and that the civilian population had ignored Israeli warnings to leave before the attack.

Israel's occupation of territories administered for nineteen years by the Arabs has defied all previous precedent. Arab civil servants, judges, teachers, and merchants have been encouraged to continue their normal lives, without surrender of responsibilities they formerly fulfilled. Schools were reopened at once and—except for certain malicious and malevolent anti-Israeli and anti-Jewish texts—the educational materials and methods previously instituted by Arab educators were retained. The government has extended economic and medical aid to all in need. Hadassah, the Women's Zionist Organization which attends especially to health problems, shipped 40,000 units of measles vaccine to Israel for use with Arab children. Farmers, tradesmen, and divided families are allowed to cross and recross the former borders freely.

True, there have been some strident voices heard among the Israelis. A small minority has expressed antagonism against the Arabs and insisted that every inch of occupied territory be retained. Far more typical, however, are the attitudes of 140 young *kibbutz* members, all veterans of the Six Day War, who gathered a few months after the conflict had ended to share reflections and opinions on the significance of their experiences. Their conversations were taped and subsequently published as a most remarkable volume called *See-ach Lochameem,* "Soldiers' Talk." This book reflects the most astonishing concerns by men who had just been through a harrowing kind of trauma. One young man, for example, reflected, "The big problem is one of education. How—despite the fact that from our point of view this was a just war—are we going to avoid turning into militarists? How are we going to retain respect for human life? . . . What we've got to avoid is cheapening life and becoming conquerors. We mustn't become expansionists at the expense of other people, we mustn't become Arab-haters. The problem is how to avoid turning our boys and our children into cynics who say, 'Justice? There's no such thing! The U.N.? Nonsense! Honor is a relative term.' The problem is how we're going to maintain our basic principles and preserve absolute rather than relative values in spite of it all."[12]

This was typical of the worries articulated by most of the participants. Another of them said, "What we have to do is try to educate our own people to behave like the boys who captured Jenin: on the same day that they saw their friends killed alongside them, they also saw long lines of refugees streaming past in cars, and they gave them water and sweets and all their food—their own battle rations."[13] Amazingly strange comment from soldiers in a victorious army! But Jews have always been a strange people, with peculiar values and goals. This is why Israel holds so much rich promise of love and of peace for the world. If it were only another small nation, a carbon copy of so many such, its preservation would be the proper concern only of its own inhabitants. It is rather the product of a people and a history which have served as cultural and spiritual yeast for all

the world; its destiny therefore remains inextricably en-
meshed with the fate of all the world.

In early summer of 1977 Israel demonstrated very dramatically its devotion to the highest ideals of universalism and peace. A group of sixty-odd Vietnamese had escaped
from North Vietnam imprisonment and were sailing in a
leaky, hazardous craft, searching for refuge. Country after
country refused their request for admission. From halfway
across the planet, from a people unrelated to them in any
way other than as fellow human beings, came an invitation
from Israel. Remembering how they themselves and their
kinsmen had so often been denied harbors of refuge during
the horrible days of the Holocaust, the Israelis reached
out with welcome and love to those who needed them.

Another sense in which Israel and the Jewish people
are vital to the search for peace relates to our need to
synthesize nationalism and internationalism. Not by surrendering national uniqueness can we learn to live together amicably any more than the individual can become
a better member of the family by forgetting his personal identity. We must learn how to become devoted citizens of our own nations, yet simultaneously citizens of the
world. Uniformity is not the road to universalism. Peace
will be realized only when each nation, while cherishing
and preserving its own special differences, respects those
of others.

In this endeavor, the Jewish people may well be a prototype. We are the only identifiable, cohesive group on
earth which exists in part as a national entity within a body
politic of its own, in part scattered among practically all
other civilized nations. We may therefore be best able to
show the way toward combining love of one's own nation
with love of all nations. The American Jew, for example,
who feels lasting loyalty to Israel, to his fellow Jews
throughout the world, and to the United States—with no

diminution of attachment to any of them, with enhanced devotion to each because of the others—has taken an essential first step on the road to permanent peace.

A final respect in which Israel holds hope for the whole world summarizes in a way its potential contributions to economic justice and to creative peace. New, more innovative concepts of religion for everyone may well issue from the sacred soil which has already nurtured so many of our noblest religious values. Some may raise their eyebrows at the thought that new religious insights may come from a nation which, as we have already observed, seems to offer the alternatives only of orthodoxy or atheism.

History can make the prospect seem less fanciful; it has happened before—and on the same soil. When Abraham first insisted that not his father's idols but an ineffable creative spirit was God, the religious experts and authorities of his time undoubtedly branded his ideas as radical heresy. When Amos and Micah proclaimed that the best way to serve God is not through the sacrificial cult but by pursuing justice and righteousness and mercy—when Hosea and Jesus understood God as the Cosmic Source of Love— they seemed to be breaking with everything the establishment of their times had called religious. Today we know that, far from being the destroyers of religion, and precisely because they were bold enough to alter the comfortable patterns of the past, Abraham and Amos, Micah, Hosea, and Jesus were prophets, creative geniuses out on the growing edge of religious truth.

I am personally convinced that no less may prove to be true of modern Israel. Its agonized spiritual turbulence, even its apparent rejection of what we have called religion in the past, may prove to be the birth-pangs of what our descendants will recognize as a higher form of religion than we have ever known. If only the world will give this infant state a chance to survive, freed of its intolerable burden of military expense, a Third Testament will come from Israel, a blessing to the world no less consequential than the first two.

The promise of the ancient prophet may yet be realized through the modern state of Israel and the worldwide Jewish people: "For out of Zion shall go forth Torah and the word of the Lord from Jerusalem."

CHAPTER THIRTEEN

Epilogue

No one in Abraham's time could have anticipated the exact nature or content of Judaism under the impact of Moses. No contemporary of Moses could have predicted with precision what the Judaism of Isaiah or Jochanan ben Zakkai, of Hillel or Akiba, would be. Judah the Prince, compiler of the Mishnah in the second century, could have foretold only in the broadest, most general terms the Judaism that would be taught by Maimonides; and Maimonides, for all his erudition and wisdom, was incapable of knowing exactly what Judaism would be in this uncertain final third of the twentieth century.

Yet threads of continuity have been woven into the fabric from Abraham—through Moses, Jochanan, Isaiah, Hillel, Akiba, Judah and Maimonides—to this very day. Though not a carbon copy, the Judaism of each age is recognizable as a legitimate issue of past periods. The adult is not just an enlarged duplicate of himself as a child. Vast change occurs, both physically and spiritually, in the course of his development; but unless a pathologically explosive eruption of personality has taken place, there is always major resemblance between what the child promised and what the adult is in process of realizing. Each of us is identifiably the continuing enfoldment of his potential in the past.

So it is with nations, peoples, cultures, faiths. Though only the rashest egomaniac would presume to predict exactly what the Jew or Judaism will be, in order to be authentic the future must be an outgrowth of the past. It is reasonable to assume, therefore, that whatever the detailed specifications, we shall continue to be a people difficult to define, combining nationalism, religion, and ethnic traits in a pattern distinctively our own. We shall persist in viewing Deity, the universe, life, and man as an essential Oneness, an Unbroken and Indivisible Unity. We shall allow neither the world nor ourselves to forget the innate potential goodness of humankind or the divine compulsion to live by our highest ideals.

Tomorrow, no less than yesterday, we Jews shall see ourselves as belonging to an especially covenanted people, partners to a contract with the Divine which is open to others too, but which we must responsibly and faithfully fulfill whether they do or not. We shall treasure and practice the rituals evolved by our ancestors as symbols of the task before us and of our bonds to all other Jews. We shall study the past, strive for holiness, affirm ourselves, respect others, apply our ethical imperatives to public as well as private behavior, see sex as a God-given good which can best be realized and enjoyed within marriage and through the family.

While accepting and promoting the integrity of all human beings and groups, we shall struggle valiantly to preserve our own identity as an indispensable prerequisite for further contributions to civilization. We shall cherish our relationship to Jews everywhere, especially those in Israel. We who are so fortunate as to live in the United States shall simultaneously cultivate our love—on different levels—for both this nation and Israel. We shall strive for justice on our own behalf and for men and women everywhere.

Some of the forms and phrases will change; emphases will be altered and new insights added. Only if the essence remains the same, however, if the broader outlines of the future are identifiable extensions of the past, will we be justified in designating as Judaism whatever the Jew practices and believes. So long as it remains Judaism, the consequences will be incalculable for all.

"Behold, My servant, whom I uphold;
Mine elect, in whom My soul delighteth;
I have put My spirit upon him,
He shall make the right to go forth to the nations . . .
He shall make the right to go forth according to the
    truth."

NOTES

Chapter One

1. *Congress Bi-Weekly* (published by the American Jewish Congress), Feb. 18, 1963, p. 9.
2. J. Cohen, *The Case for Religious Naturalism* (New York: Reconstructionist Press, 1958), pp. 164f.
3. *New York Times Magazine*, June 1970.
4. Leonard Fein, in *Moment*, July 1975.
5. Graeber & Britt, *Jews in a Gentile World*, p. 312.

Chapter Two

1. Talmud Yerushalmi, Chagigah 1:7.
2. R. T. Herford, *The Truth About the Pharisees* (Chicago: Menorah Press, 1925), pp. 36f.

Chapter Three

1. Misnah, Avodah Zarah 3, 4, 5.
2. A. H. Silver, *Therefore Choose Life* (New York: The World Publishing Company, 1967), p. 366.
3. Midrash, Leviticus Rabbah 34:3.
4. Hilchot Dayot 4:14f.
5. Responsum of Rabbi Moses Provencal, 1560.
6. M. Steinberg, *Basic Judaism* (New York: Harcourt, Brace & Co., 1947), p. 73.
7. Talmud Yerushalmi, Sotah 84.

8. M. Buber, *The Origin and Meaning of Hasidism* (New York: Horizon Press, 1960), p. 126.
9. Talmud, Menachot 43b.
10. R. Gordis, *A Faith for Moderns* (New York: Bloch Publishing Co., 1960), p. 194.
11. Talmud, Niddah 30b.
12. Talmud, Niddah 16b.
13. Tanchumah Tazria.
14. Midrash, Genesis Rabbah 11:6.
15. Talmud Yerushalmi, Ta-aneet IV:8, 68c.
16. *The Nation*, December 29, 1956.
17. H. Shapley (Ed.), *Science Ponders Religion* (New York: Appleton-Century-Crofts, Inc., 1960), pp. 80f.

CHAPTER FOUR

1. Midrash, Exodus Rabbah 47:3.
2. Abraham Joshua Heschel, *Man Is Not Alone* (New York: Farrar, Straus & Cudahy, Inc., 1958).
3. Sifre Ha-azeenu 312.

CHAPTER FIVE

1. A. R. Eckhardt, *Elder and Younger Brothers* (New York: Charles Scribner's Sons, 1967).
2. R. Ruether, "Theological Anti-Semitism in the New Testament," *The Christian Century*, Feb. 14, 1968.
3. R. Goldman, *Readiness for Religion* (New York: The Seabury Press, Inc., 1968), pp. 100, 153, 177f, 179.
4. John Haynes Holmes, *Through Gentile Eyes* (New York: Opinion Publishing Co., 1938).
5. C. Y. Glock and R. Stark, *Christian Beliefs and Anti-Semitism* (New York: Harper & Row, 1966).

CHAPTER SIX

1. Avot of Rabbi Nathan. Cited in L. Finkelstein, *The Jews*, 1:141.
2. Talmud, Shabbat 127a.
3. M. Steinberg, *Anatomy of Faith* (New York: Harcourt, Brace & Co., 1960), p. 147.

4. Rabbi Chaim Wolozhiner. Cited in *Commentary*, March 1958.
5. Midrash, Numbers Rabbah X.
6. Mishnah, Avot.
7. Talmud, Shabbat 55a.
8. *Guide to the Perplexed* 1:55.
9. Ibid., 11:25.
10. Milchamot Adonai.
11. Talmud, Baba Metzia 62a.
12. Talmud, Pesachim 25b.
13. Talmud, Sanhedrin 38a, Berachot 17a.
14. Talmud, Baba Kamma 116b, Kiddushin 20a, 22b.
15. Elie Wiesel: *From Holocaust to Rebirth*. Quoted in *Judaism*, Fall 1972.

CHAPTER SEVEN

1. 1 Corinthians 7.
2. Augustine: *De Civitate Dei* 14, 26; *Contra Iulian.* 3, 13, 27; *De Grat, chr. et de Pecc. Orig.* 2, 40.
3. *New York Times*, Sept. 21, 1952.
4. Kosnik, et al: *Human Sexuality: New Directions in American Catholic Thought*, (New York: Paulist Press, 1977), p. 29.
5. Igeret Ha-Kodesh, sec. 2.
6. Ibid.
7. Rosemary Ruether, *Religion and Sexism*, (New York: Simon & Schuster, 1974) p. 157f.
8. Robert Gordis: *Sex and the Family in the Jewish Tradition* (The Burning Bush Press, 1968) p. 37f.

CHAPTER EIGHT

1. Tosefta Avodah Zarah 2:5–7.
2. For the impact of Judaism on business practices in general, see R. Gittelsohn, *Wings of the Morning* (New York: Union of American Hebrew Congregations, 1969), Chap. 14.
3. Talmud, Yomah 39a.
4. Yalkut Shimoni on Judges, sec. 42.
5. Ibid.
6. Talmud, Avodah Zarah.
7. *Commentary*, July 1965, p. 55.

8. For a fascinating elaboration of this point, see Chapters 5, 9, and 10 of Irving Howe's *World of Our Fathers* (New York: Harcourt Brace-Jovanovich, 1976).
9. Jewish Telegraphic Agency, March 29, 1965.
10. *Scientific American,* December 1971.
11. Talmud, Berachot 59b.

CHAPTER TEN

1. E. Fackenheim, *Commentary,* Aug. 1968.
2. For further discussion of intermarriage, see R. Gittelsohn, *My Beloved Is Mine* (New York: Union of American Hebrew Congregations, 1969), Chap. 13.
3. E. W. Burgess and L. S. Cottrell, *Predicting Success or Failure in Marriage* (Englewood Cliffs, N. J.: Prentice-Hall, 1939).

CHAPTER ELEVEN

1. *New York Times,* April 20, 1969.
2. Religious News Service, January 28, 1969.
3. Maurice Samuel, *Light on Israel* (New York: Alfred A. Knopf, Inc., 1968), pp. 11f.
4. A. J. Heschel, *Israel: An Echo of Eternity* (New York: Farrar, Straus & Giroux, 1969), pp. 19–21.
5. E. Fackenheim, *Commentary,* Aug. 1968.
6. A. T. Mason: *Brandeis: A Free Man's Life* (New York: Viking Press, 1946), p. 446.
7. W. G. Plaut: *Israel Since the Six-Day War,* (Toronto: Holy Blossom Temple, 1968), p. 24.

CHAPTER TWELVE

1. *Refugees in the Middle East: A Solution in Peace* (Israel Information Services, 1967), p. 15.
2. *New York Times,* March 21, 1977.
3. *Al-Yazka* (Kuwaiti weekly), April 11, 1977.
4. *New York Times,* March 13, 1977.
5. *The Progressive,* May 1976.
6. *Judaism,* Fall 1967, p. 394.
7. *Quoted by Rabbi David Polish, in Journal of the Central Conference of American Rabbis,* June 1968, p. 19.

8. *Congress Bi-Weekly*, June 19, 1967, p. 6.
9. Jewish Telegraphic Agency, Aug. 29, 1967.
10. *New York Times*, Sept. 12, 1968.
11. *Midstream*, June/July 1968, pp. 5f.
12. Ibid., p. 21.
13. Ibid., p. 27.

About the Author

ROLAND B. GITTELSOHN, Rabbi Emeritus of Temple Israel in Boston, is chairman of the Association of Reform Zionists of America. From 1969–71 he was president of the Central Conference of American Rabbis. A graduate of Western Reserve University and Hebrew Union College, Rabbi Gittelsohn has an honorary degree of Doctor of Divinity from Hebrew Union College–Jewish Institute of Religion, and of Doctor of Science from Lowell Technological Institute. Dr. Gittelsohn has served on state and national committees on civil rights, migratory labor, and prison reform; he was also a member of President Truman's Committee on Civil Rights in 1947. Rabbi Gittelsohn's home is in Boston.